A WOMAN'S WORTH

A WOMAN'S WORTH

THE STRUGGLES AND TRIUMPHS OF A SUCCESSFUL MOMPRENEUR

Compiled by **Latrece Williams McKnight**

Co-authored by:

Latrece Williams McKnight

Reesy Floyd-Thompson

Megan Hall

Emmi Mackey

Cathy Staton

Marisa Colón

Nadine Denise Quarles

Deirdre Williams Sanderlin

Patricia Laurenceau Jean-louis

La Juan Hines Rome

Nikkia Smith

Marqueta Plum Jenkins

Mary Hazward Fernandez

Edwina V. Wilson

DEDICATION

This book is dedicated to our beautiful children who made it possible for us to call ourselves a "Mompreneur". We love you more than we can comprehend.

Lynice McKnight, Lynn McKnight Jr., Kynneth McKnight, Jenell McKnight, Simba Sanderlin, Ebony Smith, Kelly Smith, Kenisha Smith, Kelvin Smith Jr. , Riley Mackey & Blair Mackey, Carmelle Despaw, Lillian Parker, Audrina Hall & Cameron Hall, Alexis Foxworth, Xavier Evans, Joshua Evans, Tarran Evans, DeVon Staton, Terrell C. Jefferson, Shamyra Fulford, Khalil J. Rome, Jordan Rome and Logan Rome, Nivens Thompson, Jr., Porsha Thompson, Yazmine Colón, Julio Colón, Javier Colón, Selena Colón, Isbaella Colón, Tempest Quarles Brevard, Jasmine Quarles Perkins, Nicole Quarles and Karen Stancil, Jose P. Fernandez, Pablito Fernandez, Maria Fernandez, Sidvina (Vena) Lindsey, Sidneca (Sid) Lawton Dachon Negron, A'Chanti Negron, Stefon Negron, Marreon Negron, Yoshua Harris, Israel Harris, Renee Jean-Louis and Renauld Jean-Louis. It is an utmost privilege and honor for us to labor for your benefit.

We Love You
MoM

THE INTRODUCTION

———————

THIS BOOK STARTED OUT AS a way for a group of Mompreneurs, who have never been published, to share their stories.

During this time of writing we have laughed together, cried together, and made extraordinary memories together.

These pages will introduce you to some dynamic women who by no means, look like what they went through.

They will share their life with you, the good, the bad and the ugly, all in the hopes of encouraging and empowering you to push further and look deeper.

Cheers to all the MOMS out there. We have got the best jobs in the world!

CONTENTS

CHAPTER 1

LATRECE WILLIAMS-MCKNIGHT

President/CEO McKnight Williams & Associates, LLC

✴ **Who is the "Mompreneur" behind this business? Tell us about you.**
EARLY IN 1997 I STARTED La La's K.I.D.S. Inc. (Kids Into Discovering Science); a home daycare with a curriculum focused on science. I managed to do this while raising two elementary age children, with a husband working for the Military Sealift Command making frequent deployments, and keeping full time student status at the local community college. My daycare was successful from the start. It was the recipient of two grants, maintained a waiting list of over thirty children and was the neighborhood gathering spot for children.

In 2011, I began my professional coaching and consulting journey. Forming McKnight Williams and Associates, LLC was a dream come true. I always say that your biggest breakthrough comes before your biggest obstacles, AND BOY DID THE OBSTACLES COME.

My daughter, who was severing in the military, experienced severe trauma, which resulted in her being diagnosed with PTSD. I had been caring for her son since he was four months old while she was stationed in another state. This diagnosis caused my beautiful, handsome, gifted and talented two-year-old grandson to be placed in my care indefinitely. Two years after being given custody of my grandson, my daughter gave birth to a daughter. Her daughter was placed with me at 3-months-old. SO, at the prime age of forty- six, I am a mommy to a four-year-old and three-month-old.

At this point I truly wanted to give in, throw in the towel, tell my dreams good bye. I thought to myself, there is NO WAY in "HOT WATER" that I can raise two little kids and grow a business. I began to reflect on the many years of raising my two children and thought about how would have to handle it again. I began to reflect on my thoughts of being a MOMMY FIRST then a business owner. I pondered what it meant for me to be able to be the classroom parent and go on the field trips, take the left behind gym shorts to my daughter and pick up my son after practice. I had to reflect and remember how I prioritized my life. Just like the word "MOMPRENEUR", I was a MOM first and a business owner second.

After taking a deep breath and realizing that my dream didn't have an expiration date on it or an age, I sucked it up and went after it again. This time I had a plan. I made it a point to focus on these two things:

- **Message Clarity**
- **Repurposing My Business Plan Outline**

Message Clarity (KNOW YOURSELF)

To know yourself is your first priority! I HAD CHANGED. I went from an empty nest 41-year-old to a full-time mom to a toddler and an infant. How can you realistically start a business, set goals, go about life and have successful relationships if you don't know who you are or what you want? My outlook on life had totally changed. I was feeling confused. Not knowing yourself will lead to confusion and wasting much time in hit and miss situations.

To know yourself is your first priority! I HAD CHANGED. I went from a 41 year-old empty nester to a full-time mom to a toddler and an infant. How can you realistically start a business, set goals, go about life and have successful relationships if you don't know who you are or what you want? My outlook on life had totally changed. I was feeling confused. Not knowing yourself will lead to confusion and wasting much time in hit and miss situations.

When we don't know where we are headed it's hard to set goals, get motivated and determine the best course of action. Before we can do anything we must establish who we are. To know myself I had to take a real good look at my strengths, weaknesses, likes and dislikes. It was hard for me to face my weaknesses. I became afraid. Afraid of not just facing my weaknesses and afraid of failure. I felt as though I was going through the fight or flight syndrome which is when our brain interprets a situation and tells us we are in danger and we have two choices, either to stand and fight or to flee from danger. That is known as the fight-or-flight response. (lol)

What does this have to do with our weaknesses?

Well, when I took a good hard look at my weaknesses, I saw fear underlying in many of them. I had the fear of being a terrible mom and even a terrible grandma. I had the fear of wasting money on my business and disappointing my husband. I had the fear of my business failing and the people at the job I left saying, "We told you that you shouldn't have left". I had the fear of letting down my parents and myself. On many occasions, this fear is what made me flee and opt for flight.

Through mentorship from some amazing people I begin to grow and know there were ways that I could overcome fear and even turn my weaknesses into my biggest strengths.

Sometimes the only way to overcome a fear is to face it head on. This can be daunting and even frightening at first. I chose to take it slow. I began to **take small steps in the beginning which allowed me to see and recognized small successes.** Because of that I could go on to bigger and better things.

Overcoming fear is one way to face your weaknesses to find your strength.

Ralph Waldo Emerson said, "Our Strength grows from out of our weakness"

When it came time to face my fears, I took the following steps:

* **Observed and was aware of my moods, reactions and responses to what was happening around me.** This was all new to me again, raising kids, losing my freedom to come and go. I felt like I was trying to learn how to ride a bike again with training wheels. Now throw in starting a business. GEEEEEZZZZ.
* **Became aware of how these moods and emotions affected my state of mind.** I knew that when things got a little hectic and I felt over whelmed, I couldn't focus. I would go into left field. I couldn't concentrate on ANYTHING, not my home, not my business and worst of all, me

* **I examined how I interacted with others** There were so many times that I thought I was going through "the change" because I would become a mean somebody. Knowing my tone and learning how to communicate with others changed many relationships at home and in my business.
* **Observe how my environment affected me.** I began to realize that if I was surrounded by certain folk, or if I was in certain places at certain times, I felt some kind of way. I begin to examine my surroundings, evaluate my "friendships" and take inventory of my feelings. Once I deleted some folks from my cell phone and refocused on my home surroundings, I felt better. I changed my office space, added oils and scents, plants and colors. This brightened my whole mood.

After this self-examination IT WAS ON AND POPPIN! My business began to SOAR & ROAR. I remember hitting my first five (5) figure month and running through my house shouting, "I can pay my own bills this month". For so many months I had to dip into our family savings and reserves to pay for my business needs. After focusing on my message clarity and me, that's when things began to change.

I am a firm believer that your business should reflect you. If you don't know who you are you won't know your business. Imagine starting your own business and then realizing its not what you really wanted? BACK TO THE DRAWING BOARD. I'm not saying that you won't go back and change things up a bit, but at least you started out with a solid foundation. And that starts by knowing you!

The last thing I focused on to move forward was my business plan. Writing a business plan is a definite must when starting your business. You wouldn't build a house without a plan, right? Same goes for your business; no matter how big or small it is. The act of writing your business plan will create structure for implementation, keep you organized and help you overcome obstacles. John Wooden said, "If you don't have time to do it right, when will you have time to do it over?" Creating a plan will not only save you time, but save you money down the road.

In my first business plan, I was focused on a brick and mortar training facility. After acquiring custody of the two babies with NO SUPPORT, I'll talk about that in my next book "A Woman's Worth" "Grandmas' Hands" "Not Used For Just Praying Anymore, my plans had to change. I had to go back and readjust by reexamining my mission and vision statement, value proposition and sales goals. I had to be realistic. With two new little ones, the goals I had were off the charts. Running a coaching and consulting business requires a whole lot of hustle and grinding. REMEMBER THE WORD "MOM PRENEUR". I am a MOM FIRST the PRENEUR is just the way I support being financially free to be with my babies.

My Mission Statement of helping clients define and understand the purpose of their business while-giving clarity and focus to their decisions by building the leader within didn't change. My vision of wanting to enable any client to find a clear purpose in their life, release the power within them, reach their goals and fulfil their life long dreams never changed. Do you know what changed? MY HOW! How was I going to do this now with little ones? I was no longer the 22-year-old with a 13-month-old and newborn. I was a 46-year-old with bad shins who loved food and wine.

I realized the answers to my dilemmas were within me, but I needed a coach to get them out. I believe in being a product of your own product. I trust the coaching process, but it was going to cost me money that I knew I didn't have. So, all the financials adjusted and I hired coaches and joined mastermind groups.

The most valuable information I gained from one of my online business coaches, Jenn Scalia, was to truly look at your Value Proposition. A value proposition is designed to convince a potential customer that your particular product or service will add more value or better solve a problem than that of your competition. It should answer the fundamental question of "Why should I buy your product instead of your competitor's product?"

A value proposition doesn't have to be drawn out or complex, but it does need to be concise, specific and straight to the point. It needs to describe why your product is different and the tangible reasons why it will benefit your consumer.

One of the most famous and widely cited value propositions is from Domino's Pizza. They entered the pizza delivery market and knew they needed to offer a very distinct and valuable benefit to their audience in order to cut through the clutter. They knew that typically people who ordered delivery pizza were already hungry. They determined that time was also a big factor in addition to taste, temperature and quality.

"You get fresh, hot pizza delivered to your door in 30 minutes or less -- or it's free."

This value proposition in 17 words describes the benefit to the consumer and the undeniable difference between Domino's and its competitors. It definitely answered the question, "Why should I buy your product instead of your competitors?

I already knew when I was coming in the coaching and consulting business the arena was huge. I knew that my product was similar to over 50 major competitors in the market and I wondered why people would even chose me in the first place. I had my John Maxwell Certification, I was highly educated and I had corporate connections. I was ready to change the world but my business plans were interrupted for what I know was GOD'S PLAN. I was different now. With these two little ones entering in my life I had become a "Mompreneur to the second power", A SUPER SHERO. When I changed my audience changed. And so, my value proposition changed.

With two little ones, I had to get things done quickly. They demanded lots of my time! My client clarity calls went from 45min. to 30 min. What I realized was in the 30 min. time, staying focused and following my client clarity passion script, I could help my clients identify their passion connect with their purpose and create ways to make a profit!

I FOUND IT! I found my Value Proposition.

"Got 30min.? Tired of Doing What You must do instead of what you want to do? Let me help you find your Passion Connect with your Purpose and Turn your Purpose into Profit. Start making plans in 30 min to live your dreams"

Once I identified my value proposition I didn't rely on being priced competitively or getting better testimonials & referrals from my existing customers.

What I needed was a value proposition that effectively communicated how I was different.

When you are looking for key differentiators, look for:

- A clear explanation of who the product is for.
- How it is different from all the alternatives out there.
- A real reason why I should purchase from you vs. everyone else

My journey of being a Momprenuer is far from over. But over the years "both sets" of my children have **learned valuable, hands-on business lessons**. As my children and grandchildren have gotten older, we have developed such a profound level of respect for each other as it relates to my career. We discuss business and trends and logistics of events, and they bring an insightful younger perspective, often impacting the direction I may take in what I do and say. Kynneth, whose beautiful silly personality graces the cover of this book, has decided that he wants to be a Life Coach and coach his friends. He said, "Mimi, I think my friends need a "Call". I want them to know that Yes, Bad things happen, But GOOD Happens All the Time." I just started crying. He asked me were my tears happy tears and I embraced him with a big hug and said YES. I feel immense pride emanate from my children with each successful event I produce, speaking engagement that I'm at and each time I raise the bar and am acknowledged in some way. For your children to be proud of their mother's accomplishments is an extraordinary feeling.

As I continue to rear them in this business environment my prayer is that they will continue to learn valuable, hands-on business lesson. As I work to build strong individuals (MOM) and an empire (PRENEUR), I will continue to be the living examples of the following ten attributes so that they can become better leaders in their business' and outstanding individuals, in addition to being able to know what I stood for:

1: **Strength** Mommy/Mimi stood strong in the face of adversity, protecting what she believed in with heart and soul. Having conviction and sharing that sense of strength builds a unity that successful leaders have learned to harness

2: **Continuous Learning** Excellence is driven by an acute curiosity to learn and Mommy/Mimi encouraged us daily to be our best. And that's precisely why reading, training, workshops and mentorships are the key to staying competitive and maximizing your potential.

3: Integrity I want them to always hear my voice even when they are grown and far away, saying, "Do the right thing, even when it's difficult". Integrity and truthfulness are traits many leaders today lack and one that will eventually separate the great leaders from those who place less of a premium on honesty. Sadly, we see this in many political officials today.

4: Courage My prayer is for them to see that in the face of uncertainty and despair, I buckled up my boot straps and forged ahead. I want them to say, "Mommy/Mimi taught us that courage in the face of just about anything was the right course of action, and she was right. Without complaining, blaming others or hesitation, Mommy/Mimi forged ahead, courageous and proud"

5: Respect Mommy/Mimi let them in on a little secret: "Everyone puts their pants on one leg at a time". Respecting every individual in an organization from the front line to the boardroom reinforces the partnership mentality and fosters a sense of belonging.

6: Sacrifice What does real sacrifice entail? Going without for the good of another? Yes, Mommy/Mimi sacrificed for us so that we can live better, do better and want better. As leaders, there are plenty of opportunities for sacrifice, whether it's for the sake of the team, an individual employee or organization wide. Self-sacrifice is the hallmark of unselfish leadership.

7: Kindness In our home Mommy/Mimi always taught us that if you can't say anything nice, don't say nothing at all. Love your neighbor as you Love thyself. Unpleasant behavior serves little purpose and can actually detract from honest, open dialogue. Even when delivering bad news, being kind is a sign of respect and an opportunity to help others meet or exceed their own expectations.

8: Giving Back Mommy/Mimi ALWAYS teaches us that Generosity of spirit and a sense of responsibility to help others will forever define who we are. We were created to give.

9: Unconditional Love Moms need no introduction when it comes to love. As leaders, while we may not feel the same sense of adoration for our organizations, we must be passionate about what we do. Loving our work keeps us engaged, fulfilled and happy. In the same sense, we must love our employees, our customers, and each and every stakeholder that contributes to our success

10: Faith I want them to learn that Mommy/Mimi displayed unwavering confidence and assurance in GOD and her family. Having faith in your team, knowing that they are doing the right things, in the right way, builds trust. The expression: The sum of the parts is greater than the whole, is true in both life and business.

Two of the most challenging, but rewarding endeavors a person can undertake are raising a family and starting a business. Both are full-time commitments that demand a whole lot of patience, perseverance and love. Doing one or the other on its own can be difficult enough, but plenty of mompreneurs willingly choose to do both — and they couldn't be happier about it. I AM A WITNESS TO THAT!

What made you decide to start the business' that you're in?

I wanted to help myself and others like me. I wanted to be a resource to other women business owners trying to get their venture off the ground For years I did what I had to do not what I wanted to do so that everyone's needs around me were met "except my own". I felt burned out, I disliked sitting behind a desk doing accounting, I wanted to take on a new career and did not know how. All the things I want to help new women business owners through I've been through and now have found my passion and identified my purpose and have turned it into a successful coaching business.

I am adamant about not allowing other women to have to go through the challenges of being stuck, confused, unsure, unaware and feeling unworthy.

Did you know these facts?

* More than 9.4 million firms are owned by women, employing nearly 7.9 million people, and generating $1.5 trillion in sales as of 2015.
* Women-owned firms (51% or more) account for 31% of all privately held firms and contribute 14% of employment and 12% of revenues.

Businesses Owned by Women of Color

* 2.9 million firms are majority-owned by women of color in the U.S.
* These firms employ 1.4 million people and generate $226 billion in revenues annually.

Million Dollar Businesses

* One in five firms with revenue of $1 million or more is woman-owned.
* 4.2% of all women-owned firms have revenues of 1 million or more.

Statistics from Womenable report commissioned by American Express "OPEN State of Women-Owned Businesses 2015"

After doing a market analyst on my business, I knew that there was a need for my services. Out of these businesses only about 3% of them make over $100,000 a year. My company's mission is to help change that 3% to 5%.

* **What made you "LEAP"? and how did you make the leap from a secure paying job to starting your own business?**

It's better to try and fail than to wonder what might have been.

Have you ever regretted not trying something in your life? Perhaps it was trying out for the school play. or asking that special someone out on a date. That feeling of wondering what could have been might still eat at you even years down the road.

How do you avoid that feeling of regret? By trying. You don't have to do something huge, but sitting down and planning with small steps on how you will achieve your dreams will start you off in the right direction.

Little by little I forged a path towards my goals. They say the richest place on the earth is the graveyard because so many people have died with their dreams. I just refused to do that.

After a year of contemplating if I should leave my $65,000 a year, all insurance paid job, GOD begin to deal with me. I asked HIM for a sign. I wanted to know if this was truly what HE wanted me to do. After that prayer, I found things on my job becoming uneasy and overly complex. I found scandal and lies developing around me that could have ruined my marriage and reputation. That was my sign to leave.

How do you balance or how did you balance your work/home life, or is there even such a thing?

I don't believe in balance. I believe in compromise. I've totally let go of the idea of balance. At times, the housework must give. Other times the business must give. My definition of 'balance' is just to be sure everything doesn't give at once! And I've also realized that most of the time, "good enough" really is good enough. I love that I can set my own schedule, even though it's a crazy one. I operate on a 24-hour clock where I fit in all facets of my life. Some days look more traditional, 9-to-5-ish, and others flip-flop all day between work and personal responsibilities. The flexibility of being a Mompreneur helps me to be both a better professional and a better Mommy/Mimi.

What did you or what do you say to yourself when you feel like giving up? What keeps you going?

When I want to give up, I repeat to myself," It's Not About Me" and "Latrece, what will happen IF YOU DON'T DO THIS". **I also Change my thoughts.** If you believe that you cannot affect change, you will not even try. So if you find yourself saying "I can't," or "There's nothing that I can do," try changing your thoughts to "I can at least try," and "This may not work, but I'll try it." That at least allows the possibility that you can affect change.

What keeps me going is my WHY. Your "Why" is what drives you to do what you do? The reason probably isn't money -- at least it shouldn't be. There's a reason that career counselors and coaches across the country ask the same time-old question: "If money were no object, what would you do?"

"He who has a why can endure any how." -- Frederick Nietzsche

My "why" are the people whose pictures grace this chapter. Because of them, I do what I do.

* **What was the best advice you ever received? Worst advice?**

Let's start with the worst....

When I shared my vision of starting my consulting business with family and close friends they laughed or discouraged me. The words, "Do you think there is a need for this" or "Do you think people will buy this" or "Don't quit your job girl, keep working and do your "little" business on the side". I found myself internalizing those words and in turn it reflected in my business efforts. It wasn't until I got a chance to sit on a conference call with my mentor and coach Dr. John C. Maxwell, where I received some of the best advice ever. John was going over The Seven Steps to Success. He explained that the secret of your success is found in your daily routine. He stated these seven steps.

Seven steps to success:

* **Make a commitment to grow daily.** Success doesn't come from acquiring, achieving, or advancing. It comes only as the result of growing. If you make it your goal to grow a little each day, it won't be long before you begin to see positive results in your life. As the poet Robert Browning said, Why stay on earth except to grow?
* **Value the process more than events.** Specific life events are good for making decisions, but it's the process of change and growth that has lasting value. If you want to go to the next level, strive for continual improvement.

- **Don't wait for inspiration.** Basketball great Jerry West said, You can't get much done in life if you only work on the days when you feel good. People who go far do so because they motivate themselves and give life their best, regardless of how they feel. To be successful, persevere.

- **Be willing to sacrifice pleasure for opportunity.** One of the greatest lessons is: Pay now; play later. For everything in life, you pay a price. You choose whether you will pay it on the front end or the back end. If you pay first, then you will enjoy greater rewards in the end - and those rewards taste sweeter.

- **Dream big.** It doesn't pay to dream small. Robert J. Kriegel and Louis Patler said, We don't have a clue as to what people's limits are. All the tests, stopwatches, and finish lines in the world can't measure human potential. When someone is pursuing their dream, they'll go far beyond what seems to be their limitations. The potential that exists within us is limitless and largely untapped.

- When you think of limits, you create them.

- **Plan your priorities.** One thing that all successful people have in common is that they have mastered the ability to manage their time. First and foremost, they have organized themselves. Henry Kaiser, founder of Kaiser Aluminum and Kaiser Permanente Health Care, says, every minute spent in planning will save you two in execution. You never regain lost time, so make the most of every moment.

- **Give up to go up.** Nothing of value comes without sacrifice. Life is filled with critical moments when you will have the opportunity to trade one thing you value for another. Keep your eyes open for such moments - and always be sure to trade up, not down. John C. Maxwell

He had me at #3. DON'T WAIT FOR INSPIRAITION! People who go far do so because they motivate themselves and give life their best, regardless of how they feel. To be successful, persevere.

We All know the saying It takes a village to raise a child, but for a mom starting her own business, the village may be a state. So, who do you turn to or go to for help? Who are your go-to people/services?

"It takes a village to raise a child." This saying is a proverb used in a variety of African countries, which reflects the value placed on the support of family and community in nurturing and raising their children.

When Kynneth and Jenell came into my life I felt exhausted, isolated, and overwhelmed with the incredible responsibility of raising two more children in a world where I had so much going on with building a new business. I felt isolated because most of my friend's children were much older or all graduated from High School. As a children's minister and previous Day Care owner, I have a ship load of kids who love me and me them. Over the years they have grown into beautiful young adults. They are always visiting and volunteering to sit with Kynneth and Jenell so that my husband and I can get a few minutes to ourselves. BUT, there are two who have been there for me through thick and thin. Katherine Curry-Robinson (Kat) (Junell) and Mikayla Beasley.

There have been times when Kat would spend weeks with us to help. When my husband and I wanted to celebrate our 30th wedding anniversary and take a trip to Chicago, Kat moved in. We could enjoy ourselves knowing that she was taking care of our little ones and our home.

When I opened my infant care section of La La's K.I.D.S, Inc. in 1999, one of my first infants was a 6-week-old little girl named Mikayla Beasley. Watching this baby girl grow into a beautiful teenager has been a complete joy. Mikaya has become

Jenell's role model. As a Grassfeild High School State Champion Cheerleader and State of Virginia Champion Gymnast, Mikayla is everything Jenell wants to be. Sometimes Mikayla just comes by to hang out and play with Kynneth and Jenell.

When it comes to resources and services I cannot go a day without clicking on the link to these reads

* Working Mother Magazine
* Entrepreneur
* Huffington Post
* Forbes Magazine

Each of these online magazines always have such great resources and articles that I love to share with my online community as well as grab a few nuggets for myself.

What do you do to unwind and recharge? How important is this for a Mompreneur?

In the beginning, my husband supported me with taking care of the dishes, laundry, and playing with the kids which allowed me weekly consistent "Me Time." The consistent time alone allowed me to plan opportunities to include my self-care in the family schedule. (Yes, my self-care was on the same schedule with gymnastic and flag football.) What I discovered was that I became consistent at honoring me, my interests, completing the books that I wanted to read, getting my exercise in and learning so much more about the "Me" in Mommy. Today, I have a monthly membership with Massage Envy. Every month they take a CHUNK out of my business account. This forces me to go. If I'm spending money like that on massages you better believe I'm going. My husband still takes care of the dishes and laundry as well. I LOVE HIM! He knows the importance of me being able to do me.

My family is the direct benefactor of me taking time to reflect, refuel, renew and ROAR consistently.

A survey for Mother's Day 2011 from Clinton Cards says out, of the top 10 most-requested gifts, six of the 10 items involved self-care. Mothers are requesting a good nap, someone else to make dinner and clean up afterward, quality time with the family or significant other, and simply hearing their children write them a thoughtful note and say, "Thanks, Mom!"

Us Mom's Just want a break! Self-Care Is SOOOOO Needed...

The first reason that every mother needs her own "me time" is because none of us are Super Woman. It is impossible for us to deal with all of the daily demands placed on us as a wife, mother and woman without giving somewhere. After doing this day in and day out, it's only natural that we begin to feel burned out. This is generally when we get a little "cranky." I know you all know what I'm talking about. Therefore, it's important that you give yourself at least 6 hours every WEEK of "me time." It will keep you sane.

What book would you recommend for a Mompreneur just starting out? Why this particular one?
I would suggest "15 Invaluable Laws of Growth" by John C. Maxwell

My mentor and favorite thought leader John C. Maxwell published a book titled "The 15 Invaluable Laws of Growth". It is a great playbook on how to be intentional about your own personal growth. I truly believe that you cannot and will not move forward until you grow self. I want to share the super short summary of the book.

1. The Law of Intentionality
   - Growth doesn't just happen. You must be intentional about your growth

2. The Law of Awareness
   * You must know yourself to grow yourself. The first step in change is awareness, then you can change.
3. The Law of the Mirror
   * You must see value in yourself to add value to yourself. Don't compare yourself to others and limit your own self talk that is negative.
4. The Law of Reflection
   * Learning to pause allows growth to catch up with you. Peter Drucker says it like this: "Follow effective action with quiet reflection. From the quiet reflection will come even more effective action." I personally need to do more of this.
5. The Law of Consistency
   * Motivation gets you going–Discipline keeps you growing. Develop the good habits that lead to success. Just showing up is 80% of success. Some people just don't show up. You can beat them pretty easily by just being consistent in showing up.
6. The Law of Environment
   * Growth thrives in conducive surroundings. Mark Cane says: "The first step toward success is taken when you refuse to be a captive of the environment you first find yourself in." Check out my blog titled "Are you in a Growth environment." If you are always at the head of the class you are in the wrong class.
7. The Law of Design
   * To maximize growth, develop strategies. Jim Rohn says: "If you don't design your own life plan, chances are you will fall into someone else's plan. And guess what they may have planned for you? NOT much."

8. The Law of Pain
   * Good management of bad experiences leads to great growth. You must suffer pain to realize a gain. No pain, No gain. No investment, no ROI.
9. The Law of the Ladder
   * Character growth determines the height of your personal growth. Doug Firebaugh says: "Achievement to most people is something you do...to the high achiever, it is something you are." Be great!
10. The Law of the Rubber Band
    * Growth stops when you lose the tension between where you are and where you could be. W. Somerset Maugham says: "Only a mediocre person is always at his best." If you aren't stretching yourself than you aren't growing. Don't let the rubber band become limp.
11. The Law of the Trade Offs
    * You have to give up to grow up. Eric Hoffer says: "People will cling to an unsatisfactory way of life rather than change in order to get something better for fear of getting something worse." The difference between where we are and where we want to be is created by the changes we are willing to make in our lives. This is an area where I need to continue to grow.
12. The Law of Curiosity
    * Growth is stimulated by asking Why? Ask more questions. The old saying: Those who can do will always have a job, and the people who know why, will always be their boss.
13. The Law of Modeling
    * It's hard to improve when you have no one but yourself to follow. Find a mentor and look for a coach. You can't learn from someone who hasn't been there before. Find the people who have been there and done that and ask them lots of questions.

14. The Law of Expansion
    * Growth always increases your capacity. Most experts believe we only use 10% of their potential. Wow! Scary and wonderful at the same time. We all have the capacity to grow ourselves.
15. The Law of Contribution
    * Growing yourself enables you to grow others. You can't give what you don't possess. So first you must grow yourself to be able to grow others, the 14 other laws tell us how to grow ourselves.

There are a lot of little nuggets in the above text. As the last law states, my hope through my book chapter and this book summaries is to make a contribution to someone else's growth.

What are some of the ways that you involve or have involved your family in your business?

My kids Lynice and Lynn Jr., were always involved in my business at La La's K.I.D.S., Lynice was an amazing care taker and administrative assistant. Every Friday, Lynice would prepare the deposit slips for the bank. She also would help prepare snacks for the kids. Lynn Jr. was the game organizer. He had a whistle and everything. The kids loved him. During the summer, we would have theme weeks. Lynice and Lynn Jr. would help decorate and set up for the week. Lynice is an artist. She would draw everything for the center. She made the place come ALIVE!

Today, Kynneth and Jenell help me in my coaching and consulting business by being my greatest supporters (besides my husband). They chime in on conference video calls with my VA's overseas, they get out their laptops and will swear they are typing the invoices for my clients to pay.

I always ask them to draw pictures for me so that I can hang them in my office.

I'm one of those Mom's that still has every drawing their child has ever made... and I love displaying it! While you're working away, why not ask your child to draw a particular type of picture? or set them up with an art station. You can then purchase a clip-board that you can hang in your office space and display your child's latest drawings.

If you have a business that incorporates children's products in some way, you could also use their drawings as part of your branding design. Have notepads made from their artwork or even have it printed on a coffee mug.

Including personalized items from your child in your business allows them to see that they are part of it too and lets them feel more involved. Kids are always so proud of their own art-work, let them take the spotlight!

I also allow them to help with tasks like putting orders together or filing paperwork.

When I was shipping out book orders to clients, I looked for tasks that they could do. Jenell loves packing, because she gets to pop the little bubbles on the bubble wrap (so do I). For the large part, children love to help because they want to be involved. Even if it is simply putting stamps on envelopes or stacking orders in a pile. If you show them how you'd like it to be done, this can be a regular task for them.

I also allow them to be 'ambassadors'.

I encourage Kynneth and Jenell to be excited about "OUR" business. I have explained to them what I do and I let them tell other people about it. Kynneth is a John C. Maxwell quoting machine. If you ask him anything about leadership, he will let you know that "Leadership is influence, nothing more or nothing less" They love telling people about what they do to help me. Kids love helping – they really do. And they love praise and recognition. Being able to tell someone else that they helped and that they did a good job will mean they are excited about your business too.

Another way they are 'ambassadors' is I include them in the marketing side of my business. Look at the front cover of my book. Taking photos of them and sharing photos on social media of them helping gets them even more excited about being part of our business.

I am a "Mompreneur" Including them in my marketing is a must and they LOVE IT and so do I!

What did it feel like to make your first dollar as a mompreneur? How long did that take?

After I took "The LEAP" It took less than 30 days for me to received my first consulting contract. I will never forget when I got a call from a local mega church, who wanted me to help them with developing their children's ministry. When they asked my fee I almost fainted. I had been doing this for free for so long, that when a church of this magnitude called and wanted to pay me I went into shock. When I received the first installment check, I made a copy and framed it. Every once in a blue moon I take it out and just look at it and thank GOD for the process and the progress. As mentioned early in the chapter, my business began to SOAR & ROAR after a good message clarity business and self-evaluation. I remember hitting my first five (5) figure month and running through my house shouting, "I can pay my own bills this month". For so many months I had to dip into our family savings and reserves to pay for my business needs. After 18 months, I was making more than what I was making at "The Job"!...

Kids & Significant others, do and say the darndest things. Please share with us one of your funniest moments, embarrassing moments, saddest moments, and most rewarding moment that involving your family and your business?

OMG! Kynneth and Jenell are always doing something that just cracks me up. One of the most recent is the photo shot for this book and its website. I explained to them that we would be doing pictures for a book that I was going to write and that I wanted them to be a part of it. They were so excited. When the photographer arrived, and began to set up we were in the middle of breakfast. There was on piece of toast left and they were going at it because both wanted the last piece of toast. I love photographers who can capture moments. The photos you see throughout my chapter pages and on the website, are not staged. Kynneth and Jenell were just being themselves and Shavella Squire of The Photo Bizzness LLC was so understanding and knew that the most AWESASTIC pictures would come if you just let kids be kids.

What is Your Favorite Quote....

'I can do things you cannot, you can do things I cannot. Together we can do great things.' ~ Mother Teresa

Leave us with ONE WORD that you feel describes a Mompreneur?

WOW

As an interjection, it means an exclamation of surprise, wonder, pleasure, or the like:

Wow! Look at that!

As a verb (used with object) it means to gain an enthusiastic response from; thrill.

As a noun, it means an extraordinary success:

His act is a real wow.

Excitement, interest, great pleasure, or the like:

a car that will add some wow to your life.

But when you turn that WOW upside down it means ALL These things PLUS SOME, because it spells MOM

A Women's Worth Bio:

Latrece is a woman of purpose, passion and vision. She has the unique gift and ability to 'SEE' through you and walk right into your heart. She is a Certified Life Coach, Trainer and Speaker and a Founding Partner with The John Maxwell Team.

Latrece is also a member of the Forbes Coaching Council, an elite team of the world's most influential business coaches.

When working with Latrece she aims for Real Success by helping you identify your passion, connect with your purpose and turn your purpose into profit. She is the Founder and President of Real Success University, an online university equipping aspiring life coaches to reach their maximum potential. One of her favorite quotes is, " Success isn't about what you accomplish in your life, it's about what you inspire others to do~ Latrece Williams McKnight.

Below are various ways that you can connect with Latrece and learn more about what she has to offer. Join the Woman Ready To ROAR Facebook Group to ignite that ROAR in you and your business.

(888) 716-2286 toll free
(757) 576-7777 cell
Website: www.latrecewmcknight.com
Facebook: www.facebook.com/latrecewmcknight
Twitter: www.twitter.com/latrecemcknight
Linkedin: www.linkedin.com/in/latrece-williams-mcknight-56819061

CHAPTER 2

REESY FLOYD THOMPSON

Ceo & Founder at Create Good Marketing With Reesy

Who is the Mompreneur behind the business? Tell us about you.

GROWING UP THERE WERE TWO things I knew for sure, I didn't want to be a mom and I didn't want to work a regular job. I am the oldest of three girls raised by a single mom. I share a paternal bloodline with two brothers.

I'm a big picture thinker. I saw my life being completely different from everyone else's by design. I never liked fitting in, which caused me to stand out -- and sometimes not in the best way. I don't like rigid people or structures. My personality is way too fluid. I'm a raging creative. I love a good challenge. All these things most people never know because I rarely if ever let people in. I love musicals-- the gift of song. I believe many of the world's problems would be cured (or at least much more bearable) if we all had to break out in song to communicate.

I work better alone. Large groups of anything overwhelm me. I'm an introvert. I suck at networking. I don't enjoy small talk. I'm an observer. My eyes, ears, and gut feeling tell me everything I need to know. In some circles, they call this discernment and it's one my gifts. here.

I'm an empath, a feeler. I used to be ashamed of it. I've certainly been mocked for it along with being too tall, too thick, too this or that and too never quite good enough. I'm an over thinker and I dread too many options. Myers Briggs has a name for this personality type. It's INFP. It translates to Introverted, Intuitive, Feeling and Perceiving. I toggle back and forth between INFP and INFJ. "J" meaning for Judging.

I cry at the most inappropriate times. I always root for the underdog, for the people who aren't "supposed" to.

I believe in the happy ending, the fairy tale, the fantasy. My emotions are always just beneath the surface. Sometimes this gets me into trouble and sometimes it changes my world.

12 years ago, June 2005, I stood behind my husband in a Pennsylvania courtroom and watched as my life changed instantly — and changed forever when he was sentenced to 12 ½ to 15 years. I suck at math, but I knew that was a long time. At that moment, I knew everything would be different; everything would be difficult because The Keystone State just locked up the love of my life and declared he must do 100% of the minimum before being considered for release.

On the day of the sentencing, there was never a question whether or not I would keep my commitment to him; I'd made that choice before when I agreed to "until death do us part." For better or worse, I would never go back to simply being Mrs. Thompson. Now, I would also be Mrs. GE-6309.

The worst part was realizing my previous title of wife had not adequately prepared me to take on this new role as a prisoner's wife and all its complexities such as living my life as a single- married woman, running a two-income household on one paycheck, and becoming a statistic--- a cliché.

As I embarked upon what was surely going to be the hardest thing I've ever done, I look for help. I searched for resources on how to get me through this. Besides the beautiful memoir *The Prisoner's Wife* by Asha Bandele, there was no much more by way of resources. There was an obscure book or two and even organizations for families, but I wanted something specifically for the wives and partners. I wanted to know how to maintain a marriage when you're legally separated by the Department of Corrections. I craved a success story instead I was being hit with study after study saying for every year a person is incarcerated the rate of divorce goes up. One study even suggested that 80% of marriage end in divorce when a partner is incarcerated. I had at least twelve years to do. This was daunting.

I needed a light. I realized if I wanted resources, surely others needed them too given the United States prison population is over 2 million. I was going to have to create the resources.

In June 2009 (four years after the sentencing), I did just that. I set up a meet up at the local library for The Prisoners' Wives Club. All of one person showed up. She was more than enough. It felt good to talk to someone whom I didn't have to explain the nuances of this life such as getting rid of my underwire bras, carrying a stopwatch, or keeping clear purses around. She got it.

In those few hours, I knew I had the power to change my life and change my world. I didn't set out initially to start an organization and to grow it to what it eventually became but the women kept coming in person and online. That little club morphed into a nonprofit called Prisoners' Wives, Girlfriends and Partners, PWGP for short. Those four letters opened a world for faceless, nameless women who did no wrong besides loving those who society casts aside. I created resources, offered support groups and mentorship, recorded a weekly podcast, trained chapter leaders -- which afforded them all the use of the PWGP name and product materials as long as they continued to spread the word and help one more woman...no strike that...one more person because men joined too.

The exposure from PWGP opened me up to the world. I didn't know how much until I received an email through my website from someone who identified themselves as my husband's junior. The email went on to say, "I'm looking for my dad." I ignored it. One night while recording the Mrs. GE-6309 podcast, a male called in and while not revealing himself, I knew it was him-- Junior. I cut the line and later replied to his previous email, which lead to a phone call with Junior revealing that he was indeed the son of my husband. Once I saw a picture of him, it was like looking into my husband's face sans twenty years.

This man I had fallen in love with and then married without doing any due diligence had just made me a mom.

I kicked myself [hard] because in our romantic haste I never asked if he had kids and he never revealed it. Three months into our romance, two days before Christmas 2003, he was arrested. From that moment on, our lives became about the system. Everything was about the system. I love a good whodunit and here I was living in my very own crime drama.

After some long ... long ... long talks with myself, I embraced this new role. My happily-ever-after tendency skipped right over the adjustment period straight to visions of the family portrait.

I was out of my depth. I was trying to maintain a relationship with my husband in prison, while running several side hustles to fund the phone calls, while clocking in a job to keep the roof over my head, and dealing with learning there were not one but two grown children. Since I don't do anything halfway, I invited his children into my life as their stepmother, which meant I took on the responsibility to assist in their well-being.

After this revelation in 2010, six years into the marriage, five years into the sentence, I was in full super spouse syndrome and this prisoner's wife thingy completely erased Reesy. I got lost in the Mrs. Thompson, Mrs. GE yada yada, Mrs. all-things-PWGP. The girl who started it all was drowning in the life she created. While I lived my happy single-married life in the foreground, in the background my marriage was taking a hit. Years of doing the most with little was taking a toll, coupled with my newfound motherhood duties, I was navigating new terrain and my emotional GPS was way...way off.

I started to feel something I hadn't felt before. It wasn't love. It was resentment because now I yearned to have a life not tethered to anyone or anything. I yearn to know my own name. I yearned to simply be Reesy.

In addition, PWGP critics were very vocal.

Women hated me.
They hated me because I looked like them.
They hated me because I was a stain on their reflection.
They hated me because I was smart and maybe even beautiful and I "should know better."
They hated me because they feared it could happen to them too.
They made fun of me.
In their eyes, I was different *and* less. I took the stares, side-eyes and clap backs.
I bared the shame and embarrassment.
I understood, because pre-prisoner's wife, I was a hater too. The irony was not lost.
They hated me because I did the most basic thing-- fall in love with an unacceptable suitor.
I absorbed it all until finally I started to hate me too.
I was so unsure of myself.

What made you decide to start the business that you're in?
While doing PWGP, I became a marketing professional. I kept silent about who I was, after all I couldn't reveal at any staff outing that my husband was in prison. My wedding ring, which I proudly wore, revealed my marital status, but my husband never showed to any of the staff out-ings. Whenever asked about him, I spoke in the present tense because to me he was present just a few years away. That kind of inauthenticity killed any chance of developing meaningful friendships. I didn't trust anyone to let them in on it. At the time, the internet wasn't as prevalent as it is today. Even with doing PWGP, I could hide in plain sight. The truth of my life was just a Google search away, but in those days people didn't google you.

But still as my local profile started to rise, I began to pull out of PWGP.

In addition to the "normal" facade I put on every day, I was also inauthentic in my core. I worked a nine to five, but my heart was never fully in it, at least not for long. I'd hit a wall. I wanted my own thing. I wanted to be my own boss, because truth … I'm a terrible employee. Yes, I did my job and I was great at it, but every day was a struggle as my desire for more grew stronger. I didn't enjoy the hamster wheel, running as fast as you can and not getting anywhere all while enduring the nonsense of office shenanigans and politics. And an even greater truth, I don't like being told what to do.

I took any opportunity to hone my skills. I took any training that would further my life outside of the corporate rigmarole. As the world was moving online, digital marketing was trending upward. I enjoyed working in the social space because my inner introvert thrived. I love marketing. There is a lot of psychology and emotion in marketing-- understanding why people do what they do plays well with my INFP personality. It gives me an edge in creating successful campaigns. I knew anything related to marketing was going to be the key to unlock the life I really wanted.

I still didn't answer the call immediately I veered off. I started a t-shirt business to feed my raging creative, but a few months into that venture I knew t-shirts were not it. I felt my spirit out of alignment.

September 2016, I finally launched my marketing business. Staying true to my desire to create, to do good and to be good, I call the company Create Good Marketing. I teach women entrepreneurs how to use digital marketing and social media to create good in their lives and businesses.

What made you LEAP? How did you make the leap from a secure paid job to starting your own business?

What finally pushed me to make some real decisions was a forced leap of sorts. I struggled in another nine to five. Things were just not going well. Here I was with high-level marketing skills being micromanaged about basic things. My frustration showed. I gave a month's notice with the intent to have my new marketing business up and running. But, they showed me the door weeks before I was ready. Finally, I had the free time I needed.

But the joke was on me, in addition to being a terrible employee; I was also a horrible entrepreneur. Two things killed me, I needed to get out of my comfort zone and I needed to network. I've never had an issue moving product, but this was different for some reason. My introverted personality was not having it. I fell hard and fast. I had some projects coming in but not enough to live comfortably.

My business coach told me to just "tough it out." We are living in an entrepreneur's world. There has never been a better time to be self-employed. Ok... got it.

"See what you're made of." she said. That wasn't the right choice for me. Besides, I was living with a husband in prison. I knew what I was made of.

With a mortgage looming, I had to be realistic. I decided to return to the corporate world one more time. No one can decide what is right for you. For me, there was no shame in going back. I didn't feel like a failure, not in the way that I would of had I missed a mortgage payment and potentially lost my house. I work part time now so I can pursue my dream -- to give back, to serve, to change this world. That's the vision that keeps me going. I dream of a life of choice, freedom of movement, freedom to choose whom I serve, freedom to buy those darn shoes.

Giving up has never been an option because quitting is not one of the multiple choices.

My job is an investment that helps fund my business. I purposely start my day with my own work because it reminds me why I'm clocking in. It's totally mental.

Here is how I make it work:

6:00 a.m. - 8:30 a.m. - I work my business
9:00 am - 2:00 p.m. - Investment
3:30 p.m. - midnight - I chase my dreams.

How do you balance or how did you balance your work/home life?
I truly don't know what it means to have work/life balance. I think it's something people like to talk about because it's so elusive. I use one barometer to measure if I'm on track. I ask myself, "Do I feel good about the decisions I made for myself and my family?" If the answer is "yes," that's all the balance I need.

What do you say to yourself when you feel like giving up? What keeps you going?
In business, I've never felt like giving up. I've delayed my greatness in every way, it was never giving up. I lived behind the false shadow of fear. I'm in the digital marketing space; you can throw a rock online and hit tons of people in my space. I've sat on my skills eager with desire but trembling from the unknown. I'd create a huge narrative in my head about what could happen and play out that story with full reactions to things that had not yet come to pass. This is where overthinking gets me in trouble.

To every just try, there is just do. There is no fail, there are just lessons. I made a promise to a fatherless little girl who grew up with just enough to get by, a little girl who turned in a young woman who turned to every wrong in search of her inner greatness. I made a promise to that person that "one day," I would have an easier life. I keep going --- one day is now.

What was the best advice you ever received? Worst advice?
Looking to silence my inner critic, I looked for validation in what I thought was safe space. Your story makes you unique, they say. They being business coaches. Upon hearing my story in all its sorted glory, a coach very pointedly told me that no one would ever hire me as a digital marketer if they knew I was connected to prison. This threw me off track 1) Because I'd just paid someone to tell me this and 2) because deep down inside I believed it.

I allowed this horrible advice to keep me on the sidelines of my life once again. But there was another voice, a stronger, determined inner self-- that silent, not-so-silent, relentless voice I call Wonder Woman. She tells me every day. "You can do this." So far, she hasn't been wrong.

We all know the saying, "It takes a village to raise a child," but for a mom starting her own business, the village may be a state. So who do you turn to or go to for help? Who are your go-to people/ services?

I'm a researcher by nature. My favorite place to go for help is a FREE resource known as the internet. I spend hours looking for data. I love to read about my field and stay on top of the latest and greatest in talent and technology.

I get involved. A lot of my work is on Facebook. I use that to my advantage. I join Facebook group to submerge myself in communities of people who have been where I've been, communities of people who are where I'd like to be, and communities of people who I'm trying to reach.

There are a lot of business resources on Facebook. But it's not just Facebook, there a communities all over in person and on the web. Networking groups, meetups, online forums, chat rooms, business groups and yes… books much like this one are filled with people on the entrepreneur's journey.

When you are looking for inspiration to start your own business you can find people from all walks of life who have made a living for themselves in a variety of ways. Text books will have you believe that there is only one way to greatness. That is simply not true. There are an infinite number of ways to successfully master a journey. The cool thing is by reading other people's story you get a sense of what is possible. Take what is useful and applicable for you and throw out the rest. Eventually, you will create a path that is all your own.

I'm also very fortunate to have a support system that includes not only my husband and son, but girlfriends who make my heart sing. As I mentioned, I'm an introvert to I'm really bad at keeping up with people simply because my alone time is everything to me. I'm so fortunate that I have the kind of friends where we may not see each other for months or in some cases years, but when we get together we pick up like we haven't been apart. Those are the friends I've learned to cherish and they all have my back. They are super supportive and all want to see me succeed and be happy. No shade. No drama. It's all love.

What do you do to unwind and recharge? How important is this for a Mompreneur?
I'm the wrong person to ask this question. I rarely, if ever unwind and recharge. Try as I might I just can't seem to relax when there

are things that need to be done. Even when I think I'm relaxing, I'm working.

I trick myself into thinking I'm unwinding by going to a local Starbucks to work. I can sit outside and feel like I'm still apart of the world while living my laptop life.

I do enjoy binge watching Netflix and Hulu. I work sometimes with background noise. That's another trick to feeling like I'm relaxing. My husband teases me that I never really watch anything because I'm also on my laptop at the same time. If it's a really good show, I'll have a book open as well.

I have made an effort that if I'm watching a movie with my husband that I will actually put away the devices and be in the moment.

I know it is important to unwind and recharge-- all the doctors, coaches and books say so, but my brain is on 24/7, which is a good thing, a really good thing, but I find it hard to put my feet up and just chill.

I'm on a mission to create a different life for me and my family where we can kick back without worry. I'm building a life of choice.

Ask me this again in a year.

What book would you recommend for a Mompreneur just starting out? Why this particular one?
If you are reading this one, you are off to a good start. You can't go wrong with anything by Brene Brown. If I had to choose one, I would start with "The Gifts of Imperfection." So much of who we think we are (good, bad, and indifferent) comes out through our business. This book reminded me that there is no such thing as perfection and that

imperfect action is better than no action from being paralyzed with a nonexistent ideal. Everything we feel as a mompreneur is normal -- fear, doubt, comparison and it's ok. Imperfect is permission to just be and do the best you can with what you have.

What are some of the ways that you involve or have involved your family in your business?

My husband is my biggest cheerleader. He motivates me like none other. He can recount my accomplishments more than I. Whenever I'm unsure of myself or someone tells me I can't or someone doesn't agree with how I want to do something, he's right there. "Remember who you are Reesy," he says.

He's also my idea validator. I'm a serial entrepreneur. Every idea I've ever had and continue to have, he's been my sounding board. He's keeps procrastination at bay. He pushes me. When I wrote a novel (yet to be published), my husband was the one who demanded two chapters a month. When I take too long to build a website, he's in my ear. When I'm complaining about not being where I want to be, he guides me with a chant of praise, "Go Reesy, go."

The family that side hustles together stays together. Remember that t-shirt business I mentioned earlier. I wanted to completely pivot and move on, but it turns out my husband and sons are really good at it. Creativity runs in the family. Both husband and son are extroverts which means they are out front doing client acquisition. Both are great with software and conceptualizing new designs. My son is good with trends and keeping up what's happening now while my husband is good with managing the money and keeping up with expenses.

When we are out working the flea market circuit together, we all have a role to play. It takes a family to grow a business and my family is all in. This girl could not have asked for a more trust worthy side-kick or a more dedicated spawn. My mompreneur ventures are definitely a team effort. #teamthompson

What did it feel like to make your first dollar as a Mompreneur? How long did that take?
I'm totally about to date myself here, but when I made my first dollar I went into complete Sally Field mode and adopted the speech she gave after winner her first Oscar, "They like me, they really like me."

But this was the wrong approach to take and I will share why in a little bit.

I've sold a number of things candy creations, scarves, jewelry, wood signs, t-shirts, DIY workshops, and now digital marketing. These are things I've done within a 10 year period. There has been many, many more. For everything except digital marketing, within a week I made sales.

Digital marketing is different because the price point is much higher which means I have to nurture this audience. Though many marketers do it, it's not cool to ask anyone to part with several hundred to thousands of dollars quickly with a timer tick-tocking away at their freedom of choice.

Additionally, when I started selling these skills, I was unclear about whom I wanted to serve and that left me frustrated as I spoke to dozens of people only to find out they couldn't afford my services. That caused me to get clear. Once I was clear, it took two weeks to land my first dollar as a digital marketer.

Rejection is part of any business, but I've learned to rethink when I hear the word "no". No doesn't mean I'm being rejected, it means no right now-- at least not with that person.

For every action, there is an equal and opposite reaction.

I could get 9 positive reviews and 1 bad review and I will focus on the negative. "Why do you take things so personally?" I've heard this all my life. The answer is, I just do. I don't expect that to change anytime soon. I have to create a system that allows me to still be able to give to the world, but to not take in all the negative that comes with it.

I get a lot of joy from the internet, but the internet is a cruel place. If I took all the negative to heart, I would never get out of bed. Brene Brown introduced me to a wonderful quote from Theodore Roosevelt:

"It is not the critic who counts; not the man who points out how the strong man stumbles, or where the doer of deeds could have done them better. The credit belongs to the man who is actually in the arena, whose face is marred by dust and sweat and blood..."

Brene Brown takes this a step further to say, "If you are not in the arena, I'm not interested in your feedback.

When I ran PWGP, the critics were not in the arena and as I work in marketing, the critics are still not in the arena.

People are going to not like you and are going to talk about you and they will continue to do so after you leave this planet. You have to self-protect your contribution to the world. Everyone won't get it. Some won't cheer for you. Some won't want to see you succeed.

While people will buy from you because they like you, it's not a measure of your worth. I would amend Sally's now to read: "They like my work. They really like my work." Because liking me and being okay with me is up to me. No one can take that away, unless I give it to them. Now, I'm truly not interested in their feedback.

- Don't make assumptions about your audience. People give to what they find valuable. The key to weeding out those who don't is setting up a system to qualify them before getting on a call or taking a meeting.
- Money is an exchange of value. Put good into the world. Money will come.
- Money, time, and energy are all we have to give to anything. Time and misdirected energy does not replenish. Use it wisely.
- When everything is aligned as it should be, money will flow.
- Don't compare yourself to other's timing. Your timing is your own. Success isn't measured by how fast you get there.
- Measure yourself against yourself. You are your only competition.

Kids & Significant others, do and say the darndest things. Please share with us one of your funniest moments, embarrassing moments, saddest moments, and most rewarding moment that involving your family and your business?

As a stepmother, there is sense of wanting to measure up. No matter what I say or do, it's always in the back of mind that I didn't birth my children. But we don't use the word "step." My children are my children. Though I am an all-in kind of person, I realized after numerous attempts to be a Pinterest mom that my-full-grown-still-needing-and-wanting-guidance children, were ok with my just showing up. The extras were not a prerequisite or an audition to be their mom--the extras were just that--extra.

The most rewarding thing for me has been seeing my influence on my kids and knowing it didn't come from one of random articles I keep bookmarked like 25 ways to be a cool stepmom or something like that. It came from me just being me and showing them what I'm about.

When my daughter says, "Mom, I learned how to sew because of you." because she watched me sew scarves as a side-hustle. Or when she talked to me about starting an organization for her community because she watched me use my life to help others. That's love.

My son spent months with me watching me work-- seeing first hand there is a different kind of work-- different from an 8-hour day. It set a bar for things he can do in his life and it influenced him in very personal way. He started his own online sneaker company, but most importantly, our interaction set a bar for future relationships. When I asked what his girlfriend did for a living and he replied, "She's just like you. She can work from home." Mom score! Total love!

My son is now studying to be a firefighter and giving back to his community because he wants to save the world. Actually, he gets the hero thing from his dad, but looking good while saving the world--he gets that from me.

I didn't give birth to my children, but I did give birth to some of their ideas and that's been what I've needed to erase any doubt that they are mine.

All I want to do is be a good person, make my mark on the world, and know that I mattered. This business allows me to that while creating a lifestyle for my family to enjoy and a legacy for my kids to remember.

In the end PWGP was in nine states with hundreds of members brought together by a single voice. It will be rebooted this year with a new name, same mission.

Being called mom, though a role I never sought, it's a role I earned. It adds so much texture to my life.

For my husband and me, we made it to the other side and having him come alongside me in life and business makes up for years of separation.

None of this is easy, but boy has it been worth it!

I'm in the arena, and I'm here to stay.

What is Your Favorite Quote?
"If you want to live a life you have never lived, you have to do something you have never done."

Leave us with ONE word to describe a Mompreneur.
Agility

A Woman's Worth Bio
Professional digital marketer, business woman, author, founder of Create Good Marketing, founder of Prisoners' Wives, Girlfriends and Partners, and creator of Reesy's Pieces.

Reesy aka Digital Wonder Woman is on a mission to teach non-marketers and do-gooders how to use digital marketing to create good in their lives and business. She specializes in the I-don't-know-jack-about-marketing entrepreneur.

Her work has been featured on several local and national publications and she was just recently named Best Outstanding Emerging Professional and Best Social Media Personality by CoVABiz magazine.

Find her daily on Facebook creating good and sharing her best digital marketing tips with eager business owners. Wife, mother, idealist addicted to thrifting and Netflix. Super cool chick!

Join the community learning about how to use digital marketing: <u>Digital marketing for non-marketing and do-gooders</u>.

Website: Create Good Marketing
Instagram: @creategoodmarketing
LinkedIn: Reesy Floyd-Thompson

CHAPTER 3
MEGAN HALL
Founder/CEO The Inspired Women Community

Who is the Mompreneur behind the business? Tell us about you.

MY LIFE JOURNEY HAS BEEN a rollercoaster ride. In order to fully understand who, I am today we have to go back to July 3, 2010. A day that changed the trajectory of my life forever. At that time, I was engaged to be married to my middle daughter's father. We were living in a house that should have been condemned. It was not a livable home lacking heat, flooring, a stove and enough hot water for anyone to shower longer than five minutes. It was my own personal hell.

That day actually began the night before when my fiancé dragged me out of a local bar by my arm so forcefully that I could still see the outline of his hand print the next day. For years I experienced verbal and emotional abuse with him. This was the first time that the abuse extended past the verbal/emotional realm and into physical. For the next couple of hours, he screamed obscenities at me while throwing chairs and Knick knacks at my head. After he was done I started packing my things to leave.

The morning when he was sobered again he apologized for his behavior. He promised that he would never do anything like that again. It was a promise I had heard many times before. Our wedding was only a few weeks away and I clung to the belief that this time was different. He went out to run errands that morning and when he came back I realized his apologies meant nothing and his promises things would get better were just empty promises.

He came back drunk and likely high as well screaming in front of my daughters about how useless I was. His aggression didn't stop at me and soon he snapped at my oldest daughter. I immediately sent her next door to play so she wouldn't witness any more. That was when I decided I had enough of the abuse. If it was just me I would have stayed forever. I had become use to it all and had come to think I deserved it. However, I was not going tolerate the abuse being directed towards my girls.

At the time, I had no car and no license so I called my sister to come get me. She was at work but could hear the desperation in my voice so she left to come over. I didn't even know where I would live when she came all I knew was I had to leave. As I gathered my things to leave him he shot off a gun in my house. Then he ran.

I found myself trapped in my own house of horrors as the police searched for him in the woods nearby. My daughter ran over from the neighbor's house sobbing "I thought he killed you mommy." How much had she seen? How bad had it become that she hears a gun and that's her first thought? What had I put my child through? It made me realize I made the right decision even though I was homeless, unemployed, and broken with two children to care for.

The journey from homeless, unemployed, single mom of two to thriving mompreneur was a long one. It taught me so
much about life and about myself. Through
my own struggles and experiences, I am
able to help women achieve their own definition of success. Many times, it's really the
pieces of our lives that are effecting our
success.

My adversities are some of the many reasons I am the woman I am today. If I hadn't gone through all that pain I wouldn't have the resilience or the inspiration to do what I do now. To be honest entrepreneurship is not for the faint of heart. Those life lessons are what allow me to do what I do today and really under-stand the struggles other women experience.

I didn't do it all alone I met my husband only months after leaving that toxic relationship. He has believed in me from day one even when I didn't fully believe in myself. Even though in the beginning I was a mess wrestling with my own inner demons he stayed by my side. I know I am capable of doing great things on my own but his support has helped me so much!

Even with my husband support I wouldn't truly be a mompreneur without my four children. I became a mom at the age of 16 so I don't know what life or business would be like if I wasn't a mom. Growing up I never dreamed of having children or a family. Even after my daughter was born it was going to me and her against the world. So now being a mom of four has been quite an eye opening experience.

My vision when I was younger was to be a driven business women. I saw myself in power suits and running meetings. Part of that has come true along with so many other things I never even saw. I so am thankful for the opportunity to touch the lives of other women on a daily basis. All the struggles and adversities I faced were worth it if that means I can use them to guide other women.

What made you decide to start the business that you're in?
Even after marrying my husband and having two more children, twins, I was still not happy or fulfilled. I felt I should have been because I had such a better life than I did previously so I started my search. That search led me to beginning my fitness journey in 2013. I thought that would be the answer to all my pain. I was an overweight and exhausted stay at home mom. Within the six months I lost almost 60 lbs. and started feeling better but still not whole. I felt like something was missing.

A year after I started on my fitness journey I was introduced to the program PiYo and was presented with the opportunity to become a Beachbody Coach. I've always been a helper at heart even as a young child. Beachbody provided me with the opportunity not just to help but to bring in an income as well. I was sure I had found my purpose, helping people lit me up inside. Within a year I again found myself frustrated this time it was with the lack of sustainable success my clients were seeing on their journey.

Many of my clients would lose weight then gain it back then lose it again. It was a yo-yo. They never seemed to be able to see success on their health and fitness journey despite how motivated they were. I realized the problem wasn't with their motivation but disconnect within their lives. Like me they thought weight loss would bring them that feeling of happiness and fulfillment they lacked. I started to feel like I was meant for something more than fitness coaching and yearned to help women in a much deeper level.

Soon with the guidance and encouragement of some very talented women I started on a new path. That path led me to helping women with their whole lives not just one piece. Now I focus on meeting women where they are and guiding them from where they are to where they want to be.

What made you LEAP? How did you make the leap from a secure paid job to starting your own business?
I took the long way around before getting to where I want to be. In January 2011, I found out I was pregnant and a month later we discovered it was twins! At that time, my husband and I decided it would be best for me to stay home with our children. My pregnancy was high risk and with his unpredictable work schedule as active duty military we knew if I went to back to work it wouldn't work out well. Even if I could work through my entire pregnancy once the twins came I would barely bring in enough money to cover the cost of daycare for four children. It didn't seem worth it to either of us for me to work full time just to bring in a couple hundred dollars a month while our children spent time with someone else.

It wasn't long before I found myself frustrated that I wasn't contributing to the household. Guilt overwhelmed me every time I spent money on myself because I was spending but not earning. Above all I was definitely not cut out to be a stay at home mom and was stressed out daily. My dream had always been to run a company and do great things in the world. Being a stay at home mom was a far cry from that dream. That's what fueled my desire to take the leap and start my first business as a Beachbody coach.

The decision to go from Beachbody to what I do today was harder. By the time I was ready to transition I had a team of people and many clients that were relying on me. All I could think is what would people think if I stepped down. Would they think I failed? How much I would fail my clients and my team members if I stopped fitness coaching. For a while I ran both businesses but I soon realized I wasn't showing up the way I should with fitness coaching, my heart wasn't in it anymore.

After a lot of deliberation and conversations I officially called it quits with Beachbody 6 months into running my new business. I had many people who supported my decision but also had an equal amount who shunned me for it. It was a very eye-opening experience and my worst fears of failure never happened. In the end, I just realized who was really there to support me.

How do you balance or how did you balance your work/home life?
Running my Beachbody business didn't come with as much stress as running my own personal business. Beachbody had provided everything from the website to the training to the product I just needed to provide the support and "work" the business. With my new business, I had to provide it all and I had to sell myself. This added a new twist to the work/life balance.

Balancing running a business and a household has never been easy. The two go hand in hand when you're a mompreneur. When something in my life is bothering me, it can affect my business. The opposite is also true. I realized long ago that in order to have balance I have to take good care of myself first and foremost. When I am not feeling my best everything else starts to unravel too.

There are a few other things besides self-care that helps me do it all. The first is having my rules for engagement and sticking to them. Rules for Engagement are hard fast rules that include things like how many meeting I'll allow in a day and what my office hours are. They really help me decide on how to spend my time. It also makes saying no to things much easier.

Another thing I do is create a weekly schedule for myself. This helps me not forget a meeting and allows me to have time to do it all. During the office hours on my schedule I will block out times that I am going to accomplish certain tasks. I also leave extra space for unexpected things like going to get sick kids from school.

Over the years I've learned to take ownership of my own time and set boundaries so I can have some sort of work/life balance. It's imperfect and some days are better than others. When I start to feel things getting out of control I revisit my rules and see if something needs to change.

What do you say to yourself when you feel like giving up? What keeps you going?
The out of control times really make me feel like giving up. I often wonder if I am really cut out for this whole mompreneur thing. Wouldn't it be better if I just got a "real job" instead of being the one in charge? Not Really. I was never meant to work a 9-5 with someone else as my boss. Rules frustrate me especially when they aren't working and I have a hard time keep my mouth shut.

When thoughts of giving up occur I remind myself of the reasons I stayed home in the first place. Who would be the one to pick the kids up when they are sick? Me! How long would an employer be patient with that? Not very long! Then when the military moves us I would have to find a new place of employment. I really love the flexibility of working for myself.

A business coach once asked me how long I would do what I am doing if I didn't see a payout. I said, "As long as it takes." For me success isn't about money but about the lives I impact which I remind myself of when I feel like quitting. No one is an overnight success. My passion for changing women's lives fuels me every day.

When doubt creeps in I think about why I started. There is so much I want to do in life and not much of that can be accomplished working for someone else. Being a mompreneur means unlimited growth and the ability to achieve amazing dreams. When I doubt myself and my purpose I am reminded by the women whose live I've touched that I am meant to be here.

What was the best advice you ever received? Worst advice?
I would not have been able to touch those lives without the advice to just get started. When I was debating starting the business I have today I attended a local conference for women. While I was there I took advantage of two free coaching sessions. When I told them what I wanted to do both coaches responded the same way, "Why aren't you doing it already?" I told them I thought I needed a bunch of different things set up before I began. They both responded with "Just get started, the rest will happen."

The advice that has held me back the most is to follow what the "experts" in my field do. It took me awhile to realize that I didn't need to do things exactly how everyone else does it. I could receive inspiration from the actions of people in my industry but I needed to pave my own path. What sets me apart from everyone else is that I that I meet women where they are and help them achieve their own version of success. Life and business are not one size fits all so neither should our approach be.

We All know the saying It takes a village to raise a child, but for a mom starting her own business, the village may be a state. So, who do you turn to or go to for help? Who are your go-to people/services?
The women who really supported me on my journey weren't always the experts but they were the ones that helped guide my vision. Those women were never told me not to do something but instead would give me guidance on how to do it. They were the women who cheered on every success and hugged me when I failed.

My support network isn't limited to just business owners or entrepreneurs but contains women of all walks of life. Sometimes it takes an outside perspective to show you how well or not so well things are going. Having women who are willing to tell me when I am full of myself has been so important. Many times that means I need those who aren't in the trenches with me.

The women I turn to for help are always someone I trust and enjoy being around. If I don't jive with someone it doesn't matter how talented they are at what they do it never works out well. When I ask for help it's from women who support my vision and are willing to help it come to fruition. Even if that means that woman pointing me to someone who can help me when she isn't able to.

How do I meet these amazing, talented women? By putting myself out there, I've met then women in my tribe through networking events, conferences, Facebook groups, and meet ups. I am not afraid to go up to a new person and say "Hi my name is Megan. What's yours?" When I am interacting with others I always make sure to show up authentically/ I try to be more interested in learning more about them than I am telling them about me. This has allowed me to attract the right people, my people, into my life.

What do you do to unwind and recharge? How important is this for a Mompreneur?
There is no way I'd be able to show up 100% as myself in my life and business if I didn't take care of myself. Those days when I am sick or just not feeling well I clear my calendar to make time for some TLC. If I didn't there's no way people would not describe me as a positive, bubbly, inspirational person. Before I made it a habit to make time to care for myself I was the opposite of that.

For many, many years self-care was not a part of my life. Not making time for myself left me a burn out, cranky, over weight mom. That woman would not be able to the run the business I do today. She was a wreck and was struggling on a daily basis.

In the very beginning of my self-care journey I thought to take care of myself I just needed to work out and diet. I thought if I did that everything would soon be right in the world. Even after I lost all the weight I was still struggle profusely. Soon I realized that self-care was not just physical but mental and emotional; as well. I had to hit rock bottom to realize any of that.

In September of 2013 I found myself standing in my shower ready to end my life. I had a plan and I was going to make it happen. My lifetime struggle with depression had left me with this though many times before. I was not going to back out again. All the pain, hurt, and anger that I caused and I felt in myself needed to end.

What led me to this place? The night before after my husband's class reunion we went to his co-worker's house to drink and hang out. I was uncomfortable and trying to "fit in" which triggered me to drink profusely. That has always been one of my triggers. Drinking a bottle of vodka caused me to black out and vomit everywhere. The next morning, I woke up naked on the chair in my living room, my head was spinning, and I was done.

I could no longer cope with the depression I had struggled with my entire life. It was like an old friend revisiting me to validate all my woes. At that point, I was done struggling with my inner demons. I couldn't keep living with all that pain. Honestly, I thought my husband and children would be much better off without me. They deserved better than me and if I wasn't here they would be able to find someone better. That's what I told my husband when he walked in as I was preparing to end my life.

My husband sat down with the most heartbroken look on his face. He begged me not to do it. He said that my family NEEDED me. Then he asked me to do one of the hardest things I have ever done and that was so go see a mental health professional.

To be honest I was scared. I didn't want to face the things that haunted me every day. The same things that woke me up in the middle of the night screaming from night terrors. Facing those things was scary but the only other option in my mind was to end my life instead of living with them.

Seeing that counselor altered my entire life. I would not be the woman I am today without her. She supported me as I worked through everything that haunted my life. It took years of us working together. During my time with her I saw how important my mental, emotional and physical health was.

I now call it the trifecta of health. We have to take care of every piece of ourselves; mind, body, and soul. That means checking in with ourselves every day to make sure we are taken care of. If we don't first care for ourselves we can't care for those around us. That's why my health is my #1 priority. I might not do it perfectly all the time but at least I try.

In order to take care of my mental health I get in some personal development every day. That usually means at the very least reading a chapter of a book before bed. I have a stack of books on my night stand just patiently waiting to be read. There's so much I will learn from each one of them.

What book would you recommend for a Mompreneur just starting out? Why this particular one?
If there is one book I could recommend to mompreneurs or any woman for that matter it would be "You Are a Badass" By Jen Sincero. It was one of the first personal development books I ever read and it inspired me so much. I love her blunt, open nature with the use of a few profanities sprinkled in. By the end of that book I really did feel like a badass.

If profanities or blunt people are not your style I also recommend all things Brené Brown. She is such an inspirational woman who I admire greatly for her transparency and vulnerability. Her books have provided amazing guidance for me on my own journey. A personal favorite that I give away frequently is "The Gifts of Imperfection."

Books can help us learn so much about life and business. They are important tools we all need to grow, learn, and strengthen. If you're not a reader you can always get books on audio and listen to them while driving, cooking, cleaning, showering, etc.… just like you would podcast. Podcasts are also another amazing way to get in daily personal development.

What are some of the ways that you involve or have involved your family in your business?
My whole family is well aware that one of the many facets of my business is my podcast. When we do our daily dinner time ritual of asking each

member of our family what their favorite part of their day was my answer is often a fabulous podcast interview I had that day. When my children hear me listening to The Inspired Women Podcast they even say "That's mommy's podcast."

The transparency and open sharing with my family started when I realized because I worked at home my kids didn't realize I worked at all. The transition from Stay at Home Mom to business owner was seamless in their little heads. On more than one occasion they told other people "My daddy is in the Navy and my mommy stays home." I found the more I shared about my business with them the more they began to understand. When I missed an event because of a prescheduled engagement instead of saying I missed it because I was busy I would share with them what I was doing instead.

In the beginning my husband found it difficult to understand what I was doing. He didn't see the returns immediately and wondered "what I did all day." It took a lot of transparency and communication for him to understand what I was actually doing all day. He had never run a business before so I took the time to explain things to him in order for him to understand and get on board. Now he's one of my biggest supporters.

What did it feel like to make your first dollar as a Mompreneur? How long did that take?
Money has been a big part of many conversations between my husband and me. Like many people he thought if I said I was in business then the money should start coming in. It took time to explain that I first had to invest in myself and my business in order to see money to come in. Those conversations have helped immensely.

It took five months after I started my business for me to receive my first client and first payment for my services. If I'm being honest that was all because of me. During those five months, I didn't do a lot of investing my time or money in my business. The whole summer leading up to my first client was mostly spent scrolling through and posting on Facebook. I wasn't even consistent with writing blog posts or sending out weekly newsletters.

When I received my first client I was elated. Someone saw value in what I was offering. I felt like that payment finally made me an "official" business owner. When talking with other people I could now say "my client," which brought me great pride. One month after client number one in came client two, three, and four came too. Now I was over joyed to reference "my clients" when I spoke.

Growing a business is definitely a learning curve. My time with those first few clients had a lot of growing pains. I struggled to stay consistent and follow up on what I said I would do. Some of my first clients didn't show up to any of our weekly calls. I learned from that, I learned that it's has little to nothing to do with me but everything to do with them. Sometimes people have things going on that we don't fully know or understand and we just have to keep showing up anyways.

At first I didn't see the change that I was making in the lives of other women. It was like a slow ripple but months after working with my clients I began to see it. One of my clients said working with me allowed her the ability to make more in six months than she did the previous year in her business. Another client exuded so much confidence at a conference we both attended that I couldn't help but notice. Her whole demeanor was different and she said it was because of working with me.

To me the biggest reward in my business hasn't been a monetary one even though the business needs money to continue to thrive. The biggest reward was seeing the growth in my clients. I absolutely love helping them to unlock the greatness inside of them. I even find it fulfilling when I don't work with women directly but they tell me that my speaking, podcast, or my online presence has helped them immensely.

Kids & Significant others, do and say the darndest things. Please share with us one of your funniest moments, embarrassing moments, saddest moments, and most rewarding moment that involving your family and your business?

Getting so much fulfillment out of my work opens the door for me to become consumed by it. I am one of those people who can "lose me" in something I love. I'm not a think first then take action later person. I'm more of a take action now and deal with the consequences later type of person. Sometimes this can be helpful because I do things that I wouldn't do if I gave fear a moment to take control. Other times it doesn't work out so well and I fall flat on my face.

Recently my husband pointed out my obsession with my business. He said," I know you are doing amazing things and you are changing so many lives but you aren't doing what you need to do here." At first I was hurt and my ego was like who are you to tell me what to do. After some thought I realized he was right. I had stopped setting office hours for myself and I was allowing my business to bleed into my personal life.

My husband pointed out that it had been months since I really cleaned the house. He took on chores around the house in hopes that it would free up more time for me to get things done. Instead I just filled that time with more business stuff. My business and personal time had become one big blur and my family was suffering because of it.

Even though at first my husband's words had hurt it was a wake-up call I needed. I always tell my clients they need boundaries but was failing to set them for myself. Immediately I knew I had to rectify the situation so I went back to basics. Going back to basics meant not just creating a schedule that not only allowed time for both my business and personal life but sticking to that schedule too.

I didn't realize that during that time not only had I let my personal life be effected by my business but I let my personal self-care was as well. Over time I developed the habit of frequently skipping workouts and was eating more junk food than normal. My morning meditation became sporadic causing my stress levels to increase.

What is Your Favorite Quote?
Soon after my talk with my husband I reminded myself of my favorite quote "You can't pour from an empty cup." When we are constantly giving to others and not giving to ourselves we soon find ourselves burnt out. It's hard to continue giving once we've hit that level of emptiness. Both our family and our business will start to suffer.

I was reminded that I too needed to fill my cup. There's a delicate balance between business, family, and self. We have to continue to check in with ourselves so we can keep that balance. When we notice that we are struggling we have to check in with ourselves first.

Leave us with ONE word to describe a Mompreneur.
Adaptable!

We have to be able to adapt in life and business in order to achieve success. Things will come up that will knock us on our butts. Sometimes that delicate balance between everything seems to be falling apart. When we are able to adapt to every adversity and situation you will see great returns.

Remember **YOU ARE ENOUGH**!!!

A Woman's Worth Bio

Megan Hall is a life empowerment guide and speaker. By guiding and inspiring driven women, she helps them discover their own secret formula for achieving success. Megan is also the host of The Inspired Women Podcast where she connects her audience with inspirational women from around the globe and chats about topics relevant to women today. Her passions lie in connecting, guiding, and inspiring women to unlock the path to their own inner wisdom.

Megan was born and lived over twenty years of her life in a small area in Upstate NY. From a very young age she had a heart for helping and healing. Megan experienced and overcame many adversities from teen years to early adulthood while slowly losing herself along the way. A journey of self-discovery that started after her youngest children, twins, turned one brought Megan back to her roots.

Today Megan continues on her journey alongside of her husband Jeremy, an active duty Navy sailor, and their four children. Her passion for creating a more loving, kind, and empathic world is only outshined by her passion for raising happy, healthy, thriving children. Megan truly believes that life is not one size fits all. We all have something to contribute to this world and we need to stand tall in our truth each and every day.

Connect with Megan:
Facebook.com/meganhallinspired
Instagram.com/meganhallinspired
Twitter.com/meghallinspired
Meganhallinspired.com

CHAPTER 4

EMMI MACKEY

CEO At Big Kid, Little Kid Childcare

Who is the Mompreneur behind the business? Tell us about you.

ON THE SATURDAY AFTERNOON OF September 15, 1990, I was born to Reginald and Julia Mackey in the heavily military affiliated city of Jacksonville, Florida. Although not residing in the area long due to the occupation of my parents, we eventually relocated to the next duty station of Norfolk, Virginia. This is where I call home, and has been for over 24 years. For my father, I am the fourth child out of five, but for my mother I am the first born. Most of my early years it was just my mother and I as my dad was out serving the country, but this changed nine years later when my younger sister was born. It was then that I got my first glimpse of what it was like to be a mother because I was so adamant to help alleviate the stress and responsibilities from my mom that were associated with raising a child with a disability. And although it was something that I probably didn't have to do, it was so engraved in my mind that I had to.

Even amongst helping in the home as best as I knew how, I still managed to excel academically (as early as preschool) and participate in extracurricular activities. Nothing made me happier than graduating from Norview High School as number ten in the 2008 graduating class, all while juggling cheerleading, taking honors classes, working part-time, and even attending Norfolk Technical Center for Fashion Designing. Yet despite majority of my family being military affiliated, I wanted to be different and go to college. And that's exactly what I did when I enrolled into Norfolk State University on an academic scholarship majoring in Business Entrepreneurship, but later switching to Business Management. It  was throughout my college years that I experienced all the trials and tribulations life had to offer ranging from rape, mental breakdowns, and a failed relationship. My greatest joy was at the end of junior year with the birth of my first son and a restored relationship with Christ. While making the conscious decision to drop out of college after losing my scholarship, I decided to join the workforce again. Now five years later I am the mother of two handsome boys (ages 6 and 1), a full-time college student pursuing a Bachelor's Degree in Clinical/Counseling Psychology, a Sister in Christ, and the proud CEO of Big Kid Little Kid Childcare...a "Mompreneur" indeed.

What made you decide to start the business that you're in?
Now although childcare was a business that I originally never saw myself pursuing, it was something that I became passionate about over the

years. Even as a little girl it always seemed that all the younger kids would flock to me and continuously follow me around the daycare I attended. This used to drive me crazy, especially when I just wanted time to myself. Though I would not consider myself as being anti-social, I also wouldn't be the person that just walks up to an individual and start a conversation either. Yet despite my attempts to engage in other interests, it never failed that I always end up teaching or lecturing someone in one way or another. Starting as early as preschool, and sometimes even now, teachers would always use me to engage and instruct the other students or help grade papers while they focused on lesson plans. This often earned me the title of "teacher's pet" from my peers. Even with that being the situation, it was with the birth of my younger disabled sibling and realizing the struggles my mother faced in finding adequate care for her that I really began to focus on childcare in a business sense. The vision of one day operating my own alternative educational facility and recreation center for both normal and disabled children and adults alike

was an idea that continued to showcase itself in my mind. Once becoming a mother, myself at the early age of 20, I realized how many other young mothers were desperate for childcare too. Originally, I just figured I would seek employment in a childcare facility and work my way up, but to no avail this did not happen. After a few months of working in the daycare that I attended as a child, I eventually quite due to realizing the way I would run the business differed from the way the facility was actually ran. This at first became the driving force behind the start of my own daycare business, but the numerous employment rejections from other daycare facilities confirmed my entrepreneurial endeavor. Initially I began with babysitting but in order to accomplish my major goal I decided to start small with in-home childcare until I am able to one day open the educational facility and recreation center that I dream of.

What made you LEAP? How did you make the leap from a secure paid job to starting your own business?

What made me "LEAP" and how did I make the leap from a secure paid job to starting my own business? Well nothing will make a person reconsider thing in their life faster than hearing a child asking questions about why you're doing something, and facing constant rejection. When my oldest son inquired and said "Mommy, how come you're always working and we never do anything anymore," that became the initial push towards the thought of quitting my former job and starting my own business. While working for a well-known local company as a temp for almost a year, I was finally offered a permanent full-time position with the company. After accepting the offer, it saddened my spirits to learn that a week before my start date the company was experiencing an indefinite corporate freeze which would not allow me to start. No words hurt worse than hearing, "despite the situation you'll still be able to work for us as a temp and hopefully the freeze won't last long, but you would have to reapply for the permanent position and interview again." To add insult to injury I had already turned down the full-time position offered from the public-school system due to accepting the offer of employment where I was currently at. I felt betrayed, used, and underappreciated, which eventually led to my insecurities kicking back in. As if that wasn't enough, I had an ongoing custody dispute taking place where a permanent job was needed to increase my chance of ever gaining full custody back. After trying my hardest to secure permanent employment it still seemed as if nothing worked. No matter how hard I tried, every job I liked never seemed to allow me to get ahead. Still with an ongoing custody dispute, preparing for my oldest to begin kindergarten, and trying to stay afloat financially after the birth of my youngest, I decided enough was enough. I relied solely on the false promises of colleagues who mentioned they would enroll their children, obtained two prospective clients via marketing on Facebook and headed on my way to fulfill my dreams of entrepreneurship. On the eve of my 1-year anniversary of working for the company as a temp I made the LEAP from full-time temp worker to full-time "Mompreneur" and childcare provider.

How do you balance or how did you balance your work/home life?
Sometimes I feel as if there is no balance between work and home. There have been many times that I have wanted to escape from my daily work activities and go home to a peaceful environment and sleep. But this just doesn't seem to happen. Mainly because my work is at home and I am always there. Therefore, keeping a schedule is very important in my daily activities of being a "Mompreneur," especially considering the business is run within my home. The positive thing about being home based is that it allows me the ability to multi-task with things such as cleaning, cooking, homework, and other daily activities. And while being a mother is a 24/7 job I make sure to implement a vacation twice a year to spend with just my kids and family to ensure that they still receive adequate attention outside of my work environment. Most importantly I continue to pray and take time to focus on myself, whether it's a quick minute in the bathroom away from kids or a trip to the salon. Unfortunately, the alone time by myself is not often because kids are continuously with me from the time I wake up until the time I go to bed. Even though that is true, by maintaining a positive psychological well-being and healthy physical body, it makes it much easier to balance work and home life to ensure that I am able to provide for the needs of everyone, including myself. And by deciding to become a Psychology major, I have learned to implement all the lessons taught in class by incorporating them in my daily life as well.

What do you say to yourself when you feel like giving up? What keeps you going?
Even with everything going on that is positive, there are times when the thought of giving up occurs. Whenever I feel this way I remind myself of why I started in the first place – to be able to spend more time with my boys and accompany them on trips and events, to leave something behind for my family, and be able to manage my own time and determine my own monetary worth. Just the mere fact of also being able to finish all the things I once started is a source of motivation. I have always

tried to be a person who leads by example, especially for those I know are looking up to me. Never have I been the type to quit on my dreams permanently, and definitely not about to start now. Not only that, but hearing words of encouragement from other women, men, and children about how my journey of entrepreneurship encourages them to do the same and gives them something to look forward to is a constant echo of motivation. Just as I use those reminding factors to keep me going, I also tell myself that all great things take time and patience is a virtue. I know God gave me the vision for a reason and he will be with me to see it through and allow me to prosper as long as I wait on his timing. And while talking with one of my older afterschool kids, I am reminded of God's greatness and his purpose for me. If I allowed myself to give up I would not be able to show the kids that I watch that someone outside of their parents care for them nor remind them of the greatness that they have inside waiting to be unleashed. If I give up on me, then essentially, I am giving up on all those who are cheering for me as well and allowing my enemies the final say. That is something I cannot allow to happen.

What was the best advice you ever received? Worst advice?
"Have faith and trust in God!" From the mouths of both my mother and my best friend of over 13 years, this has been the best advice I have ever received. Occasionally I battle with self-doubt and often overthink and overanalyze situations to a point where I will talk myself out of many things. If I am unable to predict all possible outcomes of a situation, then it is likely I will think the risk is too great and not pursue it. Sometimes this personal trait is good, but most of the times for me it isn't.

Over the years many ventures I've felt uncertain about are times I relied heavily on my faith. If I give advice to anyone seeking to do something they are unsure about it is always, "have faith and trust God!" As I have matured I truly believe if he brings you to it, he will bring you through it. Nothing is too great for God and if as individuals we continue to seek and rely on him, he will give us all the desires of our heart. As a testament, I will never forget the day I was baptized and re-dedicated my life to Christ...it was May 2015, Mother's Day to be exact. Specifically, two weeks later I was fired from my position as a Caregiver and Nursery Assistant at a local autism facility, and the following two weeks I learned of my pregnancy with my second son. What was I going to do? From the natural eye, I was worse off now than I was before I got baptized. Why would God decide to take me through all of this right now? "He's just testing your faith now" said my best friend as I expressed my emotions to her. I experienced so much turmoil as I battled with the idea of an abortion due to unemployment and lack of housing since my lease was getting ready to expire. "Have faith and trust God" they say...and that is exactly what I did. I landed another job three weeks later, moved into a bigger place, and gave birth to a beautiful baby the following year. Now a year later I can add "Mompreneur" to the list. All it takes is faith the size of a mustard seed and trusting in God. I know now I could never go wrong if I carry that advice with me.

We All know the saying It takes a village to raise a child, but for a mom starting her own business, the village may be a state. So who do you turn to or go to for help? Who are your go-to people/services?
Something that has never been easy for me to do is ask for help. At times, I don't know if that is due to my Virgo astrological sign, my up-bringing, or just pride. The thought of appearing as incapable of accomplishing something on my own if I had to ask for help was terrifying enough to where life eventually had to humble me. After experiencing times of despair and hopelessness, I turned to God and rededicated my life back to him. Who better to guide me and provide the answers to all my questions before I even ask them? This is who I turn to first when I am in need of help. Next would be my parents because it seems no matter what type of help is needed they always have an answer, or could refer me to someone who does. But when I decided to become a mompreneur and start my own childcare business I had no immediate

family nearby and very limited monetary funds. These were the times where I realized who were "real friends" and who were "associates" …the times where it became obvious that strangers would support my business endeavor and provide information way more than those who I may have known my whole life. One thing is for sure, I had to learn to accept help when it was offered.

With that being the case, I took advantage of the resources readily available to me. Social services, the local Small Business Development Center, Child Day Home program and training centers, military bases and local business establishments became my go-to people/services. I also began using a referral system type of network. If a business errand needed to be ran, or any appointment needed to be made where children could not accompany me, it was then that I turned to the in-home childcare provider who previously watched my kids. She would serve as my backup provider in times of need and I would do the same. These types of established relationships are pivotal in the start of any business, but especially when determining its success.

What do you do to unwind and recharge? How important is this for a Mompreneur?
Imagine sitting on a rooftop gazing up at the sky and guessing what each figure is depicted in the clouds. Kind of reminds me of the little dog Snoopy on top of his dog house. This is what I would like to do to unwind and recharge. Unfortunately, this is not the case considering I would not dare take a ladder and climb on top of the roof of my house for fear of breaking my neck. Majority of the time I settle with sitting on the porch, eating a Popsicle, and listening to all of the sounds of nature. Being outside always seems to do the trick with helping me unwind from a long day of being a mompreneur. When I'm not listening to the sounds of nature, I like to listen to music ranging anywhere from R&B, Hip Hop, Country, Gospel, or Reggaeton. This

accompanied by a long relaxing spa-like bath with lit aromatherapy candles is also soothing. All of these things are essential with helping me to recharge, but what I found to be beneficial the most is planning ahead for the next day.

I have always been a creature of habit and slightly OCD. I could probably tell every detail that goes on in my daily life activities due to running on a tight schedule. Even as a pre-teen I utilized the school provided planners to map out everything academically that needed to be accomplished. Since I do not deal with change very well, this helped me to have some sense of certainty every day despite the sudden changes that may occur. In high school, I took planning to a whole other level by incorporating my dress attire for the whole week before the school week even started. This was something my best friend and I would do together as we would call each other and inform one another of the predicted weekly weather forecast so that our outfits could be coordinated. You could tell what type of week it was going to be based on our attire, whether it was casual clothes to accommodate for cheerleading practice or professional attire for a business class or job interview after school. What I have noticed is how this daily planning easily became incorporated into my adult life.

Being a childcare provider allows me to plan out weekly meals, wear a set uniform every day, and continue operating in my daily routine. As a mompreneur it is very essential that I be prepared as much as possible to reduce the amount of stress that can be experienced daily. If that means I'm cleaning at 9pm when all the kids leave so that I don't have to stress over it in the morning, or meal prepping during the weekend, then so be it. This type of planning combined with relaxation and meditation techniques allow me to unwind and recharge, after all the task of being a mompreneur is sure to throw some type of uncertain stress.

What book would you recommend for a Mompreneur just starting out? Why this particular one?

"Trusting God Day by Day: 365 Daily Devotionals" by Joyce Meyer is a recommended book for any Mompreneur just starting out. Since the days will more than likely be hectic and busy, this easy go-to book in a quick dose of daily inspiration to jumpstart any morning. Not only that, but it can be used every year since it is not specific to a certain year. Received as a gift from my mother, I recommend to any man or woman who is trying to build a relationship with Christ but feels as if they don't have the time. If paired with the *New International Version Thin Line Bible - Busy Mom's Edition*, then that is a winning combo. Nothing is better than finding good reads that accommodate the hectic lifestyle of being an entrepreneur and a mom, and those two books do just that.

What are some of the ways that you involve or have involved your family in your business?

In the words of my mother, "I have so many ideas for when you start your business." It seems as if my family had visions of me becoming a successful business owner way before I did. My whole goal when starting on the journey of entrepreneurship was to have something to leave behind for my family, as well as creating jobs for my sons, siblings, and extended family. Although this is just the beginning, I would like to have them involved in more ways than they probably know. In the future as I expand into the alternative educational facility and recreation center, I plan to utilize each individual in all aspects of the business. With degrees ranging in fields from social work, education, criminal justice and physical therapy, everyone in the family could contribute in some form or fashion. For now, I will settle with my oldest son helping in the day-to-day activities regarding the afterschool children that are watched. I also utilize him in planning activities for the kids, as well as arts and crafts suggestions that may be considered fun. Yet, I never paid attention to how much my youngest son is also helping as just a one-year old. He has been the guinea pig when implementing new techniques that would help with infants and/or encouraging kid's younger than him to become a bit more independent by following behind him. These things help make teaching and child rearing a bit easier while also showing my kids the ins and outs of the business…essentially preparing them for the workforce or operating the business when I am gone.

What did it feel like to make your first dollar as a Mompreneur? How long did that take?

How did I go from making almost $1000 every two weeks before taxes, to just $300 a week? This was a common question I asked myself every Friday as I received payments from parents when they picked up their children. Making my first dollar as a mompreneur was rewarding yet devastating at the same time. I felt so professional when writing up child-care receipts to hand to the parents, but that adrenaline rush soon wore off when the bills came rolling in. Everything I purchased to start up the business did not match the amount of money received weekly. I soon realized what people meant when saying "you have to spend money to make money." I did not break even until about five months of being in business, but even then, income received is not consistent based on the nature of my business. Yet, considering I quit my temporary job and started on my entrepreneurial endeavor of providing childcare all within the same week, it did not take long to make my first dollar. The real reward for me in regard to being a mompreneur is not based on the monetary income received, but the thanks and appreciation received for the services provided and the mere fact of knowing I am living my dream.

Kids & Significant others, do and say the darndest things. Please share with us one of your funniest moments, embarrassing moments, saddest moments, and most rewarding moment that involving your family and your business?

Many people probably wonder how the business name of Big Kid Little Kid Childcare came about. After years of brainstorming names for when I eventually went into business, nothing seemed to stick or seem fitting. It was in a general and slight comedic phone conversation with my mom that the idea originated. It was rather funny when I told her my plans to start a childcare business and the first thing that comes out of her mouth was, "girl they'll probably think you're just one of the kids and bypass you looking for the owner." Like really, of all the things to say who would've imagined that. I couldn't do anything but laugh at the moment until it actually happened. Before filing for a DBA (Doing Business As) name, I conducted parent meet and greets and that is exactly what happened...the first parent walked right past and assumed I was actually one of the kids living in my home. This gave birth to Big Kid Little Kid Childcare, not to mention the fact that indeed, most of the kids under my care are almost as big as me.

Imagine the warm day of April 21 at the city of Virginia Beach's most viewed attraction...the Virginia Aquarium. I will never forget this particular Friday, as it was Kindergarten Day and my oldest son was taking his first school field trip. This was the day I had been waiting for considering I had planned a whole month in advance and informed the parents of my childcare kids that we would also be accompanying the school on their field trip. But nothing went as planned that day. After rushing to get my son to school on time so he could go on his first school bus ride and then race home to greet all the daycare kids while packing up the SUV, it was enough to almost make me change my mind. Although I disliked not being able to take all of the kids, in order to ensure that I be able to greet my son at the Aquarium on time, I had to leave the latecomers and no-show children behind. There I was traveling with two anxious 2-year-old girls and my 1-year-old son. Everything would have been smooth if all children were in sync, but this particular day that did not happen amongst my three. In the middle of viewing the fish tank above our heads, I experienced the most embarrassing moment. Upset because we had to move on to the next area, one of my girls decides to throw a full-blown tantrum and fall out on the floor. Here I am struggling trying to snap pictures of my oldest, hold my one-year old, and deal with a 2 year old tantrum. The words that left my oldest son's mouth made me want to walk right out. As he dropped my hand and leaves me standing there he says, "Mom I'm going to have fun with my class instead, you should have just hired a babysitter to watch them" …talk about embarrassing.

Terminating childcare services for a family is never an easy task, especially once the kids have formed a bond with one another. Unfortunately, when it does happen I tell both the kids and the parents that it is strictly business and nothing personal. It broke my heart knowing that I would have to terminate my oldest son's first best friend due to his parents' financial difficulties, amongst other things. Despite breaking the bad news to them both, I decided to turn a negative situation into a positive one. I decided to throw a small surprise party on the last day that child-care services were to be rendered, but to both my surprise as well as my son's, the family did not bring their kids nor did we get to say goodbye. Over the eleven months of being in business, this definitely classifies as the saddest moment thus far.

The day every parent seems to anticipate is their child's pre-school or kindergarten graduation. Like most parents I was no different. That Friday of June 9th I got to witness my first-born walk to the front of his school's cafeteria and receive his Kindergarten certificate. The only thing that seemed to set me apart from the other overjoyed and tear-filled parents was the mere fact that I was also working. This by far was the most rewarding moment for me…to be able to attend such a pivotal event in my son's life while also emphasizing to my childcare kids the importance of education. I was still able to provide services for the parents while also showcasing overwhelming support for my son. And this was the sole goal for me as a mompreneur!

What is Your Favorite Quote?
After attending a weekend brunch with my fellow sisters so that we could all meet and get to know one another, the most marvelous bonding activity

came about. Who would have guessed that a small poster board and a few colorful markers could leave such a lasting impression in one's life? Well that is exactly what took place on that Sunday afternoon as each lady was instructed to leave an encouraging note on one another's board. It was almost like a game of speed dating with posters flying every which way as some of us wrote faster than others. After finally finishing with all ten posters and receiving my own back, something immediately stuck out to me. Not because it was the biggest or the brightest (because it wasn't), but because of the message relayed in the note written. In the words of one my fellow sisters it stated, "Though she be but little, she is powerful!" This has easily become one of my favorite quotes although it was originally derived from William Shakespeare in **'A Midsummer Night's Dream'** as he stated, *"though she be but little, she is fierce!"*

What is Your Favorite Quote?
Brave!

It is quite obvious to see why my fellow sister would write such a thing. Standing at just 4 feet and 11 inches tall, and built with a petite frame, I could easily be mistaken for a little girl and not a mother of two. Yet, despite my small stature I have always seemed to "wow" those who may have initially underestimated my abilities. Even with experiencing bullying in my childhood years I managed to push forward each day and use the gifts and talents that God blessed me with. Yes, I may be little but I am fierce and powerful indeed!

BUSINESS INFORMATON:
Big Kid Little Kid Childcare
Social Media (Facebook): www.facebook.com/bigkidlittlekidchildcare
Email: bigkidlittlekidchildcare@yahoo.com OR emmimackey@yahoo.com

CHAPTER 5

CATHY STATON

CEO & Founder MyHelpMyHope Foundation, Inc.

Who is the "Mompreneur" behind this business? Tell us about you.

IF SOMEONE WERE TO ASK me who I was 7 years ago, I would not have had an answer for them. I grew up in a home without love. As I got older I found myself looking for love in all the wrong places. Those wrong places landed me in many domestic violence relationships and in one I was raped. One day I looked up and found myself as a 21-year-old single mom working 2 jobs to make sure my son had what I didn't. This became a lifestyle for me and a nightmare for him. Working long hours and never seeing his mom. I tried to go back to school twice, but work demanded me more. I had to take care of my child. It was hard back then juggling school, my son, and being a single parent. I didn't know how to balance. The only thing that was on my mind was working to make money and making sure my son had things, when all he really needed was me. You see before the young age of 41 years old, I didn't know who I was. I simply walked around existing, broken, unaware, and uninterested in what life was and what life had to offer. I was a nobody who allowed people and things to define me. My life was headed nowhere and I had no destination in sight. Take a moment and imagine living all those years not knowing who you were. Seven years later I can proudly tell you who I am. No one would have been able to tell me that I would ever grace a national talk show stage. I sat in disbelief on the Dr. Oz stage to tell one of my stories. My organization has been named a "change maker" by Michelle Obama and Oprah Winfrey. God has blown my mind. I am before any titles a woman of God after his own heart and a champion for Christ. I am the mother of a 26-year-old handsome son who is my only child. To the world, I am known as author Cathy Staton, your self-love strategist, a Christian counselor, motivational speaker, life coach, and philanthropist. During my matriculation, I earned an AS in Psychology, BS in Christian Counseling, Life Coaching & Addiction & Recovery from Liberty University. I am the CEO and founder of My Help My Hope Foundation, Inc., a 501c3 nonprofit organization that assists women and children in crisis situations. I am the CEO of Dorcas, LLC, a coaching company that provides affordable life-coaching to those who want to reach their maximum potential. I am a woman who got up one day cut my hair off, got a tattoo, and decided that I was going to change my life because I didn't want to be mediocre anymore. I am a woman who decided that I was not the names I was called. God has showed me that I was beautifully and wonderfully made and destined for greatness. For me to be the "Momprenuer" behind the business I had to discover what made life work. Loves got everything to do with it.

What made you decide to start the business that you're in?
As a survivor of domestic violence and sexual assault God showed me how He would use my pain and turn it into purpose. He showed me that I did not go through everything that I went through for nothing. I realized that I had been broken but I was not destroyed. At the end of my abusive

married God showed me that I was going to start a nonprofit organization. I
remember the spirit leading to join the
praise dance team one day. The ladies
were showing me the steps for one of our
dances and I blacked out. I did not pass
out but I was sort of in a trance. At the
very moment was when the spirit gave
me the name of my organization. We
were practicing to a song called My Help
by Beverly Crawford. And I heard the
spirit say, "your ministry will be called
MyHelpMyHope and you will go out and

help women recover and show them the love of Christ." Then I heard my
name being called and I came out of the trance. Over the years through
my nonprofit and working with women, teens, and children, I learned that
there are a lot of people broken. There are a lot of grownups still broken
and bitter from childhood. There are many women who go through things
and they grow up or end up with a lot of emotional baggage. They are walking around with unhealed wounds and unresolved issues that are stopping
them from being who God wants them to be. I realized that I was born to
be doing exactly what I was doing. I found myself coaching women and
helping them heal from broken places. This is where my life coaching skills
come in at and why I decided to start my life coaching business. My goal is
to become a mental health professional counselor to be better equipped
to help people. I am in school for my masters in that now. We cannot lead
from a broken place. Leading form a broken place stunts growth and being all that you can be. That's why I help women recover. I want them to be
all that they can be.

**What made you LEAP? How did you make the leap from a secure paid
job to starting your own business?**
I have been in retail most of my life. I serve a short term in the United
States Navy as an Operations Specialist. When I went in I wanted it to be

a career, but God had other plans. I started at a major retail company from the bottom. I worked my way up to Assistant Manager. I gave this company 11 years of service. It was during my last two years and during my transformation that God keep telling me to "LEAP." I ignored Him. I was afraid. I was making very good money, I had great benefits, and I had job security. The biggest thing that was stopping me was the fact that He wanted me to step out on faith with my nonprofit. Let me say that again, a nonprofit. That means no profit. So, I would go back and forth with God about this. To be honest all I was thinking about was the money I would be losing. I was using half of my paycheck to help people. If I left my job I would not be able to help anybody is what I was thinking because I wasn't getting any donations and at that time I was not reaching out for help. Simply put, I was not trusting God. The "LEAP" came after I had had enough. I had been with this company for 11 years and in my last year I got wrote up 3 times. By this time, I had been promoted to a Store Planner and I was traveling overseeing remodels and store openings. I was staying in high in hotel rooms and loving my life at that time. The write ups were over very stupid stuff that you would not believe. With the last right up I had a talk with God. I asked Him what was going on. I was now on my last write up and if anything else happens I would be out of a job. I went to work one day and the morning started off terrible. I remember going to my hotel room for lunch. I got on my knees and starting praying and praying hard. It was then that I heard a tiny still voice say, "Go! Go now! I will take care of you. Just trust me." Something came over me. It was like I came outside of my body, and I watched myself pack, get in my car and start driving 10 hours to get home. As I drove, it was like a huge load lifted off me. The clouds, the trees, nothing looked the same anymore. I was like I was an angel floating as if I could touch the clouds as I drove. It was magical. It was all God. I never looked back. Since then, My Help My Hope has not only survived, but we are thriving.

How do you balance or how did you balance your work/home life?
Since my son was six months I have been a single mother. Before I learned how to balance work and home life I was all work and no play. I would see

my son in the morning and at night at bedtime. I worked day and night because I did not want my son to grow up like I did. I refused to struggle financially and be in a situation that I didn't have for me and my child. Because of this mindset, I sabotaged my mother and son relationship. Realizing this is what pushed me to learn how to balance my work/home life. This balance became difficult for me because I am a person that gives 200% in everything. I first had to pray for help to obtain the ability to discipline myself. I think discipline is the most important step to prioritizing work/home life. And discipline does not come naturally. There are so many other things that we want to do and doing what it takes to be successful and to balance life in the process takes discipline. Then I had to prioritize things in my life. I had to decide what was important and what wasn't in my personal and professional life. I had to let some people and things go. I had to find what worked for me and what didn't. After I took my leap I decided to go back to corporate America a year later and build my businesses. But this time it would be my way. I found a job that was more flexible and something that allowed me to still run my nonprofit activities and I can build my brand after work. I hit the jack pot! Not many people can say they love their nine to five. I still get to travel and make TV appearances. I have more control over what I want to do and how I wanted to do it. One day I do plan to leave corporate America permanently, but until then I am doing what I need to do to get to that place all while balancing my work/home life. I learned to say "No." I couldn't do that before. I learned that you can respectfully decline things and do it without feeling guilty. Doing this gave me more time to focus on my family and activities that brought me pure joy. I can say today that my son and I are building a great mother/son relationship. Balancing life and work also meant that I had to accept the fact that I was not Superwoman and it was okay if could not give my whole 200% all the time. If I missed something, or didn't feel like going I stopped feeling guilty because I couldn't make it. Saying "No" brought me peace. Another way I found balance is being okay if everything is not clean all the time. The kitchen and bathroom yes, but it's okay to not make the bed. I had to change thinking that everything had to be neat all the time. I would go crazy if my son had toys out of place or clothes on the floor. I learn to spend more time enjoying my life even when things got a little messy. This most important part I think to balancing life and work is me time. We have to make time to step away from our clients, the emails, social media, leave work at work, any and all distractions. Doing too much and being burnt out is no good for you or your family. Protecting your private time is essential to fully appreciating who you are and appreciating all life has to offer.

What did you or what do you say to yourself when you feel like giving up? What keeps you going?

At least once a week I want to give up. But then I remember that my relationship with Christ will bring together everything else in my life. I often talk to God about my calling. Sometimes I feel like He gave me the hardest calling in the world. And then I remember he said he would not give me more than I could bear. We all have those days where we don't want to get out of bed, when we are tired of asking for help, we are just sick and tire of being sick and tired. When I feel like giving up I sit and think about the "WHY." Two questions come to mind. Why did God bring me to this point and why am I doing this? I am reminded that God did not bring me this far to give up. Going back to your "Why" brings your clarity. It allows you to revisit your goals, re-adjust and move forward. God did not do all that He did to change my life for me to just throw in the towel. But I am human, I come close. My walk is not easy. I get frustrated and there are times when I feel like I am in this all by myself. But God always sends something or somebody my way to sway me to keep going. What keeps me going is knowing that I cannot accept my learned helplessness. When we are feeling helpless we must make every attempt to climb out of the pit of despair even when we feel alone. Another thing that keeps me going is accepting the fact that some things will get tough. Everything will not be easy and everything that I am going through is preparing me for what is coming. The feeling of giving up will come and go but I have learned to be happy and persistence. Persistence and knowing God is with me every step of the way keeps me going. Knowing who I am and the "WHY" keeps me going full speed ahead. Never give up.

What was the best advice you ever received? Worst advice?

I remember when I first started my organization and being overwhelmed about the lack of support. My first few events I would be in tears because I none of my so-called friends and supporters were coming out to my events. None of the support was past a social media like and that is not support. I was sharing this frustration with a deaconess at my church and I will never forget the advice she gave me. She told me to "let it go." I didn't want to hear that but it changed my life and the way I would ever think about supporters and having any event. She told me to stop worrying about who shows up and who doesn't show up at my events, and to just do what God tells me to do. She said my biggest support would come from God and strangers. And she was right. Since then it doesn't matter if one person shows up at my event or 50 I carry on as if it was God sitting in the audience. I have learned that quality is better quantity, and that purpose will always beat popularity. God had one more thing for me to deal with and that was support from my own church. I just could not understand why my own church would not support my efforts. This was something else that ate at me on the inside. I would hear and see my colleague's churches supporting them, but I couldn't fig-ure out what I was doing wrong and why I couldn't get support. On my way to an event God told me, to continue to focus on Him and Him only and to go to church for fellowship and the Word. I couldn't figure out why this was placed in my spirit until I got to this event. During the event, I sat at a table and did not know anyone. We spoke, and shared what we did and how we knew the event organizers. No one at the table knew anything about me. After the event a man sitting at my table, who happened to be an apostle, asked if he could speak to me. He introduced himself and held my hands and told me God told him to tell me something. Now I am not big on peo-ple coming up to you and telling you God told them to tell me something. Some people are false prophets. I must protect my anointing. He began saying that, "God told him to tell me to "let it go." "Let go of thinking your church is going to support you." "They are not. Just keep doing my Will." As this man spoke, tears fell from my eyes like a waterfall. At the very moment, I knew this was not a false prophet that this was real because this man didn't know me. How could he know what was tearing me up on the inside? It was all God. You see what I had inside of me was stopping God from using me. The worse advice I was ever given was to not open up a domestic violence shelter. Had I listened to them I would have lost the building that was given to me to open one up. Never listen to naysayers.

We All know the saying It takes a village to raise a child, but for a mom starting her own business, the village may be a state. So, who do you turn to or go to for help? Who are your go-to people/services?

Immediately, I use to go to family or friends for help. I learned to not do that anymore. My first instinct is to turn to God for help. I pray and ask God to help me and to send the right people to me to help me get what I need done or to help me do what He would have me to do. It is sad to say, but people will let you down. Once He shows me the way, I follow His lead in who to reach out to. It depends on what I need help with. I could be something I just need to get off my chest and I talk to Him and then the Holy Spirit may lead me to talk to a friend. There have been times when I needed financial help and my father or a friend was there for me. If it involves my business, I email or call my coach. When it involves my nonprofit, it truly does take a village. I reach out to the community. Sometimes I won't get any responses at all and then God will make a way. I truly depend on God for all my needs and continually pray He sends the right help. All help is not good help. Being a mom and raising a child you have to have people you can depend on. It is always good to have people in your life that you can turn to for the help you need.

What do you do to unwind and recharge? How important is this for a Mompreneur?

To unwind and recharge I may take a day just to myself, spend time with family, or a girl's trip. I meditate, pray, or I may read a good book, or exercise. I also like to window shop, get my feet or hair done. It is very necessary for a mompreneur to unwind and recharge. Finding balance allows you to function better in every area of your life. When you balance your life, it keeps everything in your life and business fun and achievable. It is also very important to be consistent one you find a healthy way to unwind and recharge. Some of the things you choose to unwind and recharge may not have to be done every day, but make sure you do something for yourself. It is necessary to evaluate often if you are stretching yourself and being okay with stopping it. People may think we are super woman but we can't be everything to everybody. As a mother, we do have to be everything to our children, but value yourself and how you spread yourself between family and other activities.

What book would you recommend for a Mompreneur just starting out? Why this particular one?

For a Mompreneur just starting out I recommend "Good Enough Is the New Perfect: Finding Happiness and Success in Modern Motherhood." I recommend this particular book because it is a about new mothers who learned how to balance their business and being a mom and they are winning. The book is about moms who changed their mindset to learn how to be happier, more confident, more successful, and no two stories are alike. It is the perfect map for learning how to balance a career and family.

What are some of the ways that you involve or have involved your family in your business?

I have involved my son in my nonprofit. He has helped set up for events and distributed toys, food, and clothing to those in need. Whenever we are doing anything for the community I invite my family to assist. I think it is important to get the family involve so they can see what you do and how much work it takes. I think them seeing also helps them to understand why you do what you do.

What did it feel like to make your first dollar as a Mompreneur? How long did that take?

When I made my first dollar as a mompreneur it felt unreal. I celebrated and praised God over and over again. I couldn't believe that people truly loved my vision. To me it already wasn't work because it was my passion. But making that first sale gave me so much hope. I told myself over and over again that I could do it! It didn't take that long at all because I had been wearing my products, and advertising. People were already in love with my tee-shirts. It was just a matter of marketing them right. My biggest joy came when I had people order from other states. That blew my mind to thing that someone was going to be wearing one of my shirts on the other side of the world. Then came my book sells, products, and more. Doing what you love to do and making a profit is the perfect example of God turning your pain into gain. Not just for money, but also to help people who need you the most. Seeing everything you work hard for such as your web site, social media pages, etc., take off and you get profit in return is a great feeling. Trying to build a business as a mompreneur, especially as a single mompreneur takes a lot of time, sacrifice, and hard work. Seeing your dreams come to life before your eyes is a miracle. God gets all the glory.

Kids & Significant others, do and say the darndest things. Please share with us one of your funniest moments, embarrassing moments, saddest moments, and most rewarding moment that involving your family and your business?

Yes indeed, children say the darndest things. This story is both funny and embarrassing. I borrowed a pair of my girlfriend's shoes before. My son must have been about 5 years old. The shoes were red and really pretty. I kept the shoes for about a week and then I returned them. One day my son had a doctor's appointment and when we got there my friend happened to be there with her son as well. She also had the red shoes on. As my son and I are waiting my friend was checking in. I spoke to her and my son turned to look. As he looked he yelled "mommy she has your shoes on, tell her to take them off" and he started crying as well. I could not believe it. I explained to him that they were her shoes not mine and that I only had borrowed them. It was very embarrassing. Another time my son and I visited a new friend I hadn't too long met at home. My friend and I were sitting and talking. He wandered off in another room. A minute or two later we hear someone running down the hall and he's yelling "mommy it stinks in there" while pointing. I was so embarrassed; I never took him there again.

One of the saddest moments for me was learning that my son had Type 1 diabetes. He had worked so hard in ROTC and had plans to go into the air force. About 6 months before joining he broke his patella playing basketball. He had some complications and ended up being hospitalized and that is when we found out he had diabetes. We were devastated. Over the years this has been very hard for us both to deal with. Before he turned 18 years old I was able to monitor, cook for him, and make him eat the right kinds of food. Since then he struggles with eating and talking care of himself. I pray for him daily because even now at the age of 26 years old he still doesn't understand how serious his condition is. I have tried everything to help him to understand. It has been a very hard thing for me to deal with as a mom seeing your child sick. This is where I put my faith in God again. Another sad moment was losing my mother. We didn't have a great relationship when I was growing up, but her last 7 years we started getting closer. I always wanted that mother and daughter bond. She was close with my son and he took it hard. That is why it is important to me to be a chain breaker in my family. I want to show my family what love is because we didn't have it growing it. I think my parents did they best they could with what they were taught. My father wasn't in my life growing up. Today my father and I have a great relationship that grows day by day. Family is important and I want to teach that to our next generation.

One of the most rewarding moments for my family is seeing me break our generational curse with abuse and education. My family seeing my nonprofit thrive me graduate, was life changing. Domestic violence was a generational curse for my family and God used me to say no more. We don't have many college graduates in our family. I only know of two relatives. Growing up abused and being bullied made me hate school. But God had other plans. Graduating with three bachelors at one time changed the game for family and women mompreneur. I plan to put my degrees to work to help many people. You can do anything that you want to do with the right balance, discipline, focus, and determination.

There are so many rewarding moments in my business. I would say seeing the face of people you have helped brings so much joy. Helping that person get to that next level or helping them get unstuck and you see them afterwards and priceless. I get the same joy with my nonprofit. Seeing the eyes of a child light up who thought they weren't going to get anything from Santa clause is so rewarding. Helping that mom get school uniforms for her children after leaving a domestic violence situation does something to you. I love what I do. Many people cannot say that. Every day I get to wake up and walk in my God given purpose. There is nothing like it. It took me a while to get to this place. No more chains. Life is what you make it. You only get one chance. Live every moment, laugh every day, and love beyond words.

What is Your Favorite Quote?
"We make a living by what we get but we make a life by what we give."- Winston Churchill

Leave us with ONE word to describe a Mompreneur.
"Survivor"

A Woman's Worth Bio
Cathy Staton brings with her over 20 years of leadership development experience. Cathy is an author, Christian counselor, motivational speaker, philanthropist, and life coach. Managing a successful nonprofit and teaching cutting edge life skill strategies join uncompromising integrity as the hallmarks of Cathy's service. As an author and speaker, Cathy has a passion to tell her story and share the tools she used to not only survive, but thrive. A self-published author and more importantly a "survivor" who provides messages of hope, inspiration, humor and encourages people to find their voice and use life's stumbling blocks to rebuild their own lives. She is the CEO and founder of MyHelpMyHope Foundation, Inc., a 501c3 nonprofit organization that assists women and children in crisis situations. She is the CEO of Dorcas, LLC. Dorcas

provides affordable life-coaching to those who want to reach their maximum potential. Through one-on -one coaching, group coaching and custom presentations, she uses proven techniques to help people find fulfillment in their lives while doing what they love. Cathy is the recipient of the Wavy TV Channel 10 Who Care Award, the Zeta Phi Beta Sorority, Inc. Finer Woman Award, Hampton Roads Gazeti Exemplar Award, ACHI Magazine Woman of the year Award, and the Garden of Hope Unity Award from Gethsemane Community Fellowship Church, among others. Cathy's work has been featured on many television stations such as Tribune Media and Media General, and the Dr. Oz Show. Cathy has also been featured in publications such as the Virginia Pilot, and the New Journal and Guide, the Gazeti, and Tidewater Women, to name a few. The My Help My Hope Foundation was recently selected as a changemaker by Former First Lady, Michelle Obama, and Oprah Winfrey. During her matriculation Catherine has earned an AS in Psychology, BS in Christian Counseling, and BS in Life Coaching & BS in Addiction & Recovery from Liberty University.

Facebook: @authorcathystaton, @myhelpmyhopefoundation
Instagram: @authorcathystaton @myhelpmyhopefoundation
Twitter: @cathystaton@myhelpmyhope
Periscope: @authorcathystaton
Websites: www.cathystaton.com, www.lovesgoteverythingtodowithit.com, myhelpmyhope.org

CHAPTER 6

MARISA COLÓN

Director Of Sales And Operations Tru Vizion Solution

Who is the Mompreneur behind the business? Tell us about you.

THE FUNNY THING IS, SIX years ago, you never could have convinced me that I would be a mother or an entrepreneur for that matter! So, sitting here as a mother of five, writing a book about my journey as a Mompreneur, is UNBELIEVABLE to me! I am pinching myself right now to make sure I am here; I mean really here, in the present, this is my reality!

To paint the picture of how I made it here, let's back it up a few years to where this journey began. In the fall of 2011, I was coming out of a long relationship, where I had spent years convincing myself that

that relationship was meant to be. By the end of it, I was emotionally drained, I felt like I had failed, and I could not see the future clearly. I had not been true to myself for years because I was trying to force a relationship to work, not knowing that I had no idea what real love was. The love had fizzled out of that relationship way before the end; it just took me so long to realize it because I wanted it to work more than anything I had ever wanted in my life up until that point. Going through this process of telling my story, reminds me of how out of line my priorities were in life.

The only thing that was keeping me going during this time was my commitment to my career. This was the one place in my life that I could see results and success based on the effort that I was putting in. I had worked hard in other areas of my life, but just like the relationship I was in, it didn't matter how hard I worked, nothing ever changed. I started working for this company in an entry level position, and climbed my way up to being a store manager. I loved leading people, creating a space where the team thrived, and working together to achieve success. I felt like this was my purpose. I was able to impact my team by inspiring and coaching them to reach their goals personally and professionally. I am extremely competitive, so winning with my team was an amazing rush! I always preached the message of work life balance, but in reality, I had none. Work was my life. That workaholic mindset did not end here, but this is where the shift began.

One night, my best friend Shannon and I decided that we needed a night out. I was stressed from all of the relationship drama, and she was going through a tough time where her mother was hospitalized for an extended amount of time. We needed to get out, get a few margaritas in our system, and just unwind. We ended up at a Mexican restaurant right before they closed. While we were sipping on our jumbo margaritas, we noticed the waiters were starting to break down the tables and move the chairs in the dining area we were sitting in. I remember asking the waitress if we needed to hurry up and leave since they were closing. She explained that they were preparing the dance floor because they had Latin dancing on Friday and Saturday nights. We had our fair share of tequila at that point, and were completely ready to stay and dance our cares away! Now let me add a quick side note, my Dad's family is Mexican, and growing up I had always felt disconnected from that part of my culture. To add to it, I had always dreamed about being a Latin dancer. With all the liquid courage in my system, this was the perfect night to let my dreams live!

This is my husband Julio's favorite part of the story, so I will tell it from his perspective. He says that I gave him the nastiest look ever, and he stopped my friend by saying, "What is wrong with your friend? Why did she give me such a mean look, do I owe her money?" She laughed hysterically, knowing that I have resting bitch face, and told him to talk to me. Shannon and Julio are two peas in a pod. They are two of the funniest, no filter having, and craziest people that I know, so of course they hit off their lifelong friendship instantly. The night was full of laughing and dancing, and it was exactly what I needed. I felt like I was on Dancing with the Stars as Julio was teaching me how to dance Bachata. I had the hottest, smoothest, Puerto Rican dance instructor, and you couldn't tell me I wasn't a professional dancer at that moment.

As the night was drawing to a close, Shannon told Julio, "Marisa can't stay out all night; she needs to get home to her son." She was setting him up, but he played right in to it! "Oh, she has a son?! I have two kids at home also!" Shannon was talking about my fur baby, Romo! She has a unique way of getting people to open up and share information, without them realizing what she is doing. The laughs continued, and when Shannon was ready to call it a night, Julio and I weren't quite ready to part ways. We walked around the fountain near the restaurant, and talked for hours. I know this sounds crazy, and you only hear about this type of stuff in movies, but I know now that God brought us to that place on purpose. Our meeting was ordained. We would not have crossed paths any other way. We weren't each other's "type", but we learned as the journey continued that we were exactly what each other needed.

When I finally met Julio's kids, Yazmine and Julio, I fell in love with them instantly. They were both so full of life and personality, just like their Daddy. Julio was raising Yazmine and Julio as a single father after his marriage with their mother ended. I could write another whole book about children and their perseverance, but I will just say that watching the evolution of this family has been amazing to say the least. They have inspired me with their love, strength, ability to forgive, and resilience. Somewhere along my journey, I had convinced myself that I would never have kids of my own. Maybe because I had never had a "pregnancy scare". Maybe because I was a career obsessed workaholic and I could not imagine how I could do that with kids. Maybe, I didn't think I would be a good mother. Whatever it was, I convinced myself it was not meant to be. I remember telling Julio as our love grew, that my heart was so full of him, Yazmine, and Julio. I shared with him how perfect our readymade family was, based on the belief that I would never have children of my own. From the beginning Yazmine and Julio were mine. I have never thought or labeled them as anything else. It was perfect. I was engaged to marry a man that loved me more than I had ever been loved before. I was learning to love in ways that I never knew were possible. I was starting to renew my relationship with God. And, on top of all of that, I was continuing to reach new levels of success in my career.

In January of 2013, I had reached a new high, and one of my greatest career accomplishments. I was promoted to a District

Manager, and had a territory that included 6 stores, and a team of 130! This is what I had worked so hard for; and the crazy thing was that right beyond my excitement, was a mountain of fear. For the first time, I was nervous about my abilities, and doubt was creeping in. My mentor, best friend, and previous boss helped get me back on track like she always did. This is where I started to learn that the things that scare the crap out of you are the exact things that you need to do. On the other side of fear and doubt, is the opportunity to stretch beyond what you believe is possible and that is where real growth happens. So, this next year was going to be exhilarating as I stepped in to that growth, but I was ready!

Three weeks in to my new role, and right after paying for my wedding dress, the most unexpected thing happened. I was pregnant! My husband has dreams, and these dreams always come true. Just before that he told me that he had a dream of me holding a baby girl that looked just like me. I remember calling him to tell him I was pregnant, and I started the conversation with "Your words are so powerful! Now I am pregnant because of your dream!" You want to talk about being scared; this is where life got real for me. I had no idea how I was going to make this Mom life work with a baby! Not only was I worried about how I would take care of a baby, I had no idea how I was going to be able to work, AND I still wasn't married. Not how I pictured life. As the pregnancy was drawing to a close, I had to start making arrangements at work for someone to step in to my role while I was out for three months. This was a huge challenge for me. The thought of turning my team over to someone else was unimaginable. Remember, I am a control freak, so I was obsessed with what would happen with the progress our team had made, the results we had achieved, and the thought that this person could come in and actually do a better job than me. The fear and doubt crept in again, but I knew I had to just believe that everything was going to be ok. I reassured my team that I would still be checking in, and I wanted them to call me if anything major happened while I was out. I was setting the expectation in my mind that I was going to continue to be involved and not loose complete control while I was out.

After 48 hours in labor, a baby in distress, and a worn-out mommy; Javier came in to this world via cesarean. Once I looked at Javier for the first time, life immediately started to fall in to place. I loved him beyond what I ever could have imagined. When we finally made it home, I was so wound up in being a new mommy, I did not even have the brain power to think about work. It was the craziest thing to comprehend. I enjoyed my three months off, stepped in to my Mommy role completely, and enjoyed every minute. Okay, well maybe not every minute. By the end of it, I was ready to go back to work and get back to the hustle. I missed my work and my team. I was blessed to have my best friend's mom watching Javi when I went back to work, and I learned quickly that she would spoil and love him just like her own.

Now here is where the craziness starts. Javi is about seven months old, our wedding is two months away, and I find out I am pregnant... again! I was in total disbelief! I was just getting life in order with three kids - how in the world was I going to balance four? Julio and I were married in August. I knew I was marring the best husband and father. He was beyond what I ever could have imagined for myself. By the grace of God, I survived another pregnancy while working and juggling my responsibilities at home. Selena was born in February of 2015 and my heart grew again when I saw her beautiful face. This maternity leave was very different. By that time, we had transitioned Javi's Nany in to our house to be there with the older kids after school. While I was home with Selena, she was able to help me balance taking care of Javi, who was almost a year and a half. This maternity leave was WORK!! A toddler and a new born was no joke. This was my new life. I don't know what I would have done without the help during the day, and the older kids on duty to help at night.

On Halloween of that year, I found out I was almost three months pregnant with number five. When I told Julio, he thought I was joking. We just stared at each other in disbelief. Please understand, we love our kids more than anything in life, but four kids was tough!! I was working a ton of hours as usual, but for the first time I was battling with feeling guilty about not working more and not spending enough time with my family.

Another piece of information that I haven't shared is that Julio was an entrepreneur. Before I met him, he and his brothers owned a security contracting business. The business had grown from selling monitoring services and doing handyman work to fill the gaps to a steady stream of commercial and residential work and subcontracting for larger companies. I was always proud of his dedication to running his own business and this was my first example of what real faith was. Julio started his business after taking a step of faith to follow a vision that God gave him. Taking that first step was huge and it was amazing to see where God brought them from and to see where he was taking them as their business continued to grow.

When I was preparing to have Isabella in April of 2016, I felt like I was a professional at walking away from work and starting fresh when I returned from leave. In three years of being a District Manager, this was my third maternity leave. It was a running joke at this point. Everyone just sat back in awe, wondering how I did it all. From the outside view, I was a respected, highly motivated, results-driven, successful leader. I had a glamorous life, an amazing job, the perfect family, and beautiful home. The reality was, I was stressed out and walking on a thin line of sanity trying to be the perfect leader and mother. The control freak in me was losing it… and the mad woman with extreme rage was coming out more often. The ones that suffered the most in this time were the ones that I loved the most - my family. I would find myself coming home from work and snapping at the littlest things. What do you mean the house isn't cleaned? And homework isn't done? I remember being in the final months of pregnancy with Bella and in one of those moments of rage, I swung a broom at our family pictures on the wall. Glass went everywhere, and my kids just stood there crying and screaming. I was so overwhelmed by life that I lost it because there was a mess on the floor, and my husband was standing up for the family as I was raging about who was going to clean it up. Hearing him defending everyone else, and not me, sent me over the top and I lost it. Completely out of line and unacceptable behavior. Immediately after, I was in tears from shame and guilt. I knew I could not continue like this... not for my family... and not for me.

This last and final maternity leave, I spent a lot of time thinking and praying for God to show me what to do. As much as I loved my career, and as successful as I was, I knew it was taking a toll on my family and me. It wasn't that I did not have the skill or ability to continue, the issue was that my priorities were out of line. The struggle to balance was destroying me. Reflecting on my life, I can see all the times that my priorities were out of line, God would force me in to situations where I realized how much I needed Him. Somewhere along the line, God's sense of humor kicked in and hit me. Here is the woman that never thought she would have kids, with five kids. The control freak and workaholic was being forced in to a situation that I could not control, or work my way out of. I finally realized that God was moving me down a path that He called me to, and I was going to have to trust Him and give up control. If I would have continued to fight, I could see how the story would have ended. Our Nanny would be raising our kids and I would probably end up in a mental institution for losing my mind. As I prayed and looked for direction, it finally started to come in to focus. I was blessed with a large family, because God choose me to be their mother. That was the ultimate responsibility that was being overshadowed by my career. And of course, I needed to be able to contribute to our household financially. Instead of working my life away for corporate, God was showing me that I could use my skills and talents to help my husband and his brothers take our family business to new levels of success. We would be able to streamline our efforts, and reach the full potential of what God promised Julio in the beginning.

This was the hardest decision that I have ever made in my life, but I can say now, that taking the step of faith and becoming a Mompreneur has been a complete blessing.

What made you decide to start the business that you're in?

For my initial jump in to the entrepreneurial world, I did not have to start a business on my own. Instead, I was coming in to a business that was operating and making money, but never had a foundation that would be scalable for us to reach our full potential. My husband and his brothers started the business a few years before we met. He and I would have conversations nightly, running down the happenings of our day. He would ask me for advice and I would offer my opinion to help him work through new opportunities or challenges he was facing. When we decided that it was time for us to join forces to grow the business, the main goal was for me to create the necessary structure so we could hire employees and ultimately win larger contracts.

I came to the table with years of business and leadership experience, which was quickly put to the test when I entered this new world. I was used to corporate structure, designated partners, and standard operating procedures. Now, I had to teach myself about business taxes and finances, entity types, how to build a website, and a variety of other topics that I had never experienced. The hardest part of the transition was that I did not have any partners to lean on like I was used to in my old world. Thankfully, I stumbled upon Peninsula Women's Network, and the connections that I made helped me navigate the challenges I was facing. Not only did I meet some phenomenal partners for our business, but I was finally able to connect with women that were walking the same path of business ownership and balancing that life with strong family values. I cannot say enough about the amazing friendships I have gained on this journey, and I honestly do not know where I would be without these ladies.

In this past year, I have gained a tremendous amount of business knowledge that you can only truly understand as you walk the path of an entrepreneur. I am not going to sugar coat anything, we have faced some major challenges in our business, and I have had some personal struggles with the Momprenuer life. The most exciting part about all of this is, in the most challenging moments, I have uncovered more insight in to my true purpose and calling. Even as I sit here sharing my story, I am working on some major shifts to start my own business ventures as I continue to support the growth of my husband's business. I know now that God was moving me in to a place in life where I could have more clarity and connection with Him so that He could guide my steps in to the future. If I would have stayed tied to my old career, I never would have seen the purpose He had for my life and family. I know that I am called to help other Mothers embrace their journey, and to empower entrepreneurs to follow their dreams.

What made you LEAP? How did you make the leap from a secure paid job to starting your own business?

I gave you all a sneak peak in to how my life was right before I made the jump. I was at a crossroad, trying to figure out how I was going to give 100% to my family, while trying to make a living that would support us now and in the future. Once I felt the pull to help my husband with his business... I spent a month in prayer, waiting to hear God tell me what to do. During that time, a few things happened.

I was sitting at my favorite car wash place, and I grabbed a magazine while I was waiting. The very first page had a letter from the editor where she told the story of her friend that left a six figure salary to pursue her passion in art and comedy, and she lived a life where she was happier than she ever could have imagined. I knew immediately that was God speaking to me. I was struggling with that exact same story. I was making a six figure salary, but I was not happy. I could hear God telling me not to worry about the money, and by setting that aside I would find true happiness.

I was not sold that easily, so I went home and worked our family budget to the dime. I was going to be taking a substantial pay cut, and that was hard to swallow. I went line by line to see what expenses we could cut, and what was a necessity for us to maintain. I was going to have to make some sacrifices personally, like start doing my own manicure and pedicure, and stop shopping at will. As a family, we would have to limit out meals out, and start cooking more meals at home. After all the number crunching, I found a way to make the budget work, and I knew the sacrifices were going to be worth the peace that would come.

After that, I saw a message from Steve Harvey on TV about jumping. In that message, he talks about how every successful person has had to jump at some point in their lives. If you have not heard this message, I strongly encourage you to go find the video and watch it! The part that resonated with me was that if you stay on the ledge, which is safe, you will never soar. The only way for you to soar, is for you to jump off of the ledge. Here again, I knew this was God telling me to get over the fear and doubt, and just trust Him. He was calling me to soar like the wings of eagles, and I was going to have to jump.

When I picked up the phone to call my boss to tell him that after 10 years I was resigning, I was sick to my stomach. I loved my job, I loved my team, and I knew the experience that I had gained was going to set me up for success as a Mompreneur. As soon as I got the words out of my mouth, I felt instant freedom; chains of bondage were being broken. In that moment, I knew my life was going to change forever, and I was ready for all God had in store for me and my family.

How do you balance or how did you balance your work/home life?
There is no such thing! Ok, ok, there is such a thing, but the concept of balance is nothing like the fake lives that you see on most social media!

Balance is something that I have always struggled with, and I have recently learned why so many of us struggle with it. We are trying to create balance by mimicking what we see our friends, sisters, or co-workers doing.

We look at social media and see these perfect pictures of working moms coming home, cooking a picture perfect dinner, in their perfectly clean and beautiful homes, with the smiling faced kids, and we think that is the way it is supposed to be. The picture of balance that we see creates huge problems for us. First, it is a glimpse in to one moment in time. Second, no one shares the pictures of the chaos that was going on while they were trying to cook that picture perfect meal. And three, every family is unique, so creating balance will never work with a cookie cutter approach!

I attended a conference where a couple spoke about their approach, and it was the first time that the idea of balance cliqued for me. This couple owned a few different businesses, and they had three children. This is important to me, because if I am going to take advice from someone, they need to be walking a path similar to mine. The way that they create balance, was to set boundaries on the non-negotiables, and stick to their schedules as much as possible.

Here is what that looks like for my family, and how we make it work. My husband works late most nights and travels at least a few days per month, sometimes more. I can be more flexible with my schedule because I can choose to work during the day or catch up late at night. The non-negotiables for us: we have dinner as a family at least two nights a week, Sunday is church and family day, and we take at least two family vacations per year. To some, this may not sound like we spend a lot of time together as a family, but for us we know this is the bare minimum of time that we will spend. On a good week, we may be together for dinner five times, and we may have activities and events on the weekend where we get to hang out together. On the other hand, on a rough week, where we are running in a hundred different directions, we know that we will have dinner together twice and Sunday family day is a guarantee. Those boundaries help to keep us grounded and we know it is the best we can do right now. As the kids grow, and our lives shift, the non-negotiables may change as well and we will always make sure we are giving the family the time that is needed. The other important piece of this is that these boundaries help to reduce frustration, especially on my part. If I expected my husband to be home seven days a week for dinner, and he was running late, inevitably I am going to be frustrated. If I know that I have him guaranteed on two nights, and if he can make it early a few other nights, then we look at it as a bonus and everyone is happy.

From a scheduling perspective, I take care of all of the kid's doctor appointments and extra-curricular activities, and my husband and I schedule in our own personal time into our days. He knows if he wants to work out, he needs to get up early in the morning to make it happen. I know that I need to schedule all of my personal and work time between the hours that our Nanny is with us, or understand that the only other time I have is after the kids go to sleep, and that means less sleep for me. I have learned not to set myself up for failure, like saying I am going to work out in the morning before the kids wake up. I know that the minute I get out of bed to start that process, the kids will wake up, my plans will be ruined, and I will start my day on the wrong foot. All of the routines that we have in place have been from trial and error, so we learn what works and try to stick with it.

The funny part of this balance piece is, my husband and I have completely swapped roles over the course of our relationship! When I was the one working a million hours, he had the more flexible schedule and was the first one home every evening to cook dinner and start the nightly routine. We have learned to respect and appreciate each other's contributions, and we understand that we are a team and we have to support each other. It has not always been easy, especially at the end of a long day, but we both know what is like to be on the other side so we have more compassion on those rough days.

The other piece that I have to mention for our family is that our older kids help out A LOT! They are amazing and are the best big sister and brother in the world. For example, bed time is a family affair every night. They help bathe the three little ones and get them to sleep like clockwork. During the day, they help out every time we ask and they are so committed to helping that most times we do not have to ask. So understanding all that they do, I have committed to making sure they get their own personal time as well. I work really hard to make sure we let them spend time with their friends, do activities they enjoy, or just have alone time. Their balance in life is just as important as ours.

What do you say to yourself when you feel like giving up? What keeps you going?
I can hear the self-talk kicking in as I read this question, and let me tell you, it happens more often than we would probably like to admit! The truth is, if this entrepreneur life was easy, then everyone would be doing it.

I can think of two times right off the top of my head where I was ready to throw in the towel. One situation was driven by our financial situation and the other had to do with a misalignment of vision between my husband and his brothers. In both situations, the thoughts running through my head were the same. "Why am I dealing with this unnecessary stress? I can just go find a job and not have to deal with this headache!"

Here is the reality - I may not have to worry about money or alignment if I went back to work for another company, but there would be plenty of other points of frustration for sure. Looking back at my career with corporate, there were plenty of situations where I was under pressure, faced challenges, and felt extremely frustrated. In those situations, I never said to myself, "I am just going to quit." Instead, I buckled down and found a way to overcome the obstacle. Some situations were more difficult than others, but I have never been a quitter. I have always given my all and made adjustments when necessary, even if I had to change something about myself or learn something new. In all of the challenging situations I can remember, I know that I experienced some type of growth as I worked through them.

So how does this keep me going? I know that I am going to face obstacles and challenges whether I work for myself or for someone else. What I lose by going to work for someone else is what I have found to be the most important. I would lose the ability to put God and my family as top priorities in my life. I would lose the ability to create a flexible schedule to live life on my terms. I would lose the ability to follow the purpose that God is showing me for my life. And while these may not be driving factors for the next Momprenuer on the brink of giving up, that is what keeps me in *purposeful* hustle mode.

What was the best advice you ever received? Worst advice?
I have been blessed with amazing mentors and role models in my life that have provided loads of great advice. I want to learn as much as possible from other women that have already paved the way so that I can avoid unnecessary bumps and bruises along the way.

One of the women that I met on this journey, and now one of my very close friends, saved me from losing it one evening with just a few simple words. I had spent hours preparing an agenda and content for a company meeting with my husband and his brothers and I was going to be leading the meeting. I had arranged to use an office space that my friend had access to so this was on a whole new level from the restaurant setting that we had in the past. I was super excited, because I was going to be sharing some significant achievements that we had made, and we were planning a brainstorming session to create strategic plans to help push us even further ahead. To make a long story short, wires were crossed regarding the time of the meeting. No one showed up except for my husband and me. I am an over communicator, so I know I told them about the meeting seven different times, seven different ways. My friend was doing me a favor and it took some extra coordinating to get the office space for the meeting. Now, I was going to have to call her after all of that extra effort to tell her we were not able to have the meeting. I was completely embarrassed. Here I am, trying to build new connections and make our family business look official and we cannot even get everyone to the meeting without issues. Plus, I had spent so much time preparing and now I felt like it was all wasted effort. When I picked up the phone to call her, I was frustrated and this was one of those moments where I was asking myself, "What the hell am I doing?" She listened to me vent, then she calmly said, "Marisa, remember why you started. Remember your purpose." That was exactly the advice I needed to ground me. Not only did it help bring me out of the frustration in that situation, but I remember that advice every time I face the challenges and frustrations that make me question what I am doing. I knew when I committed to helping our family business grow it was going to require patience and a strong mindset. The guys were making money and growing before I came on board, so I was not coming in to rescue them from failure. Instead, I was coming on board to help them level up; shifting their mindset, creating structure and foundations for growth, and partnering with them to manage their business with a scalable model. These changes were not going to happen overnight, and I had to learn to work with them on a different level. I am not the boss in this scenario like I was used to be in my past life, so I have had to flex new muscles to ignite the changes that needed to happen. No matter how frustrated I get in the moment, I understand that with every struggle there is an opportunity for new learning and growth. The struggles do not change my purpose, instead they show me what adjustments I need to make for the future.

I could continue this story with other examples of great advice and lessons that I have learned over and over again, but I hit a wall when I tried to recall the worst advice that someone gave me. Since my brain is already overloaded, I must have subconsciously removed the bad advice from my memory bank! I am pretty solid at detecting BS, and as I explained before, I do not entertain advice from people that are not walking on the same path as me. So with all of that being said, I am sure I have been given advice by someone who meant well, but I just smiled and let the advice go in one ear and out of the other. That is a lesson learned in itself. I think too often we rely on advice from others, instead of trusting our own instincts. The answers that we need are already within in us, we just need to listen and trust the process. As mothers, when it comes to our children we know them better than anyone else, so we need to trust that pull in our hearts that tells us what to do. The same applies to our businesses, marriages, and any other relationship or situation for that matter. The advice that we cling to is generally because it lines up with what we already know, we just need someone else to reassure us that we are making the right decisions. I can remember facing challenges and going to my girlfriends for advice. The most impactful conversations happened when they asked me questions that forced me to dig inside for my own answers. It is easy for someone else to tell you what to do, but it is nowhere near as powerful as recognizing that we have all the answers that we need. Confidence and trust in ourselves is most often the missing piece.

So I will close with a piece of advice for each mompreneur out there: Choose carefully who you lean on for advice, and trust your own instincts to guide your decisions.

We All know the saying It takes a village to raise a child, but for a mom starting her own business, the village may be a state. So who do you turn to or go to for help? Who are your go-to people/services?
My support system is, hands down, the best! First of all, I have an amazing husband that is also the best Dad in the world. Our situation is unique since we are in this entrepreneur journey together and I believe it makes us that much stronger. Coming in at a strong second is who our kids call their nanny, Nana. That tells you how much love they have for each other. They are her grandkids at heart. She was already extremely

supportive while I was in my corporate role, even staying overnight when both Julio and I were traveling. Now that I have made the shift to a Mompreneur, our bond has grown even stronger. I work from home, so of course I am way more involved in the day to day then I used to be when I left the house for ten to twelve hours a day. She is my right hand. And saving the best for last, my mother and sister are always available whenever I need them! They know me better than anyone, so they know when I am at my limit and they fill the gaps for me every time. Having five kids, and three under four years old, adds a whole new dynamic to asking for help. I have a hard time when I am by myself with all of the little ones, so I often feel guilty asking someone to take on that responsibility. It is hard work! I find myself not asking for help most times and I sacrifice things that I would like to do because I know being Mommy is my priority. I know that they will only be this young for a short period of time and it will get easier as they grow and become more independent and self-sufficient. So for now, I take the help when I can get it, and I do my best to enjoy the time I have with them while they are young.

Because I understand the challenges first hand, I have a huge passion to help other mompreneurs. I recently started a new journey as a Chapter Leader for a networking and education organization for Mom Entrepreneurs, Business Among Moms. In addition to connecting with other successful mompreneur CEO's on a professional and personal level, most of the events are kid friendly, so it is a win, win, situation. (Professional, personal, family)!

What do you do to unwind and recharge? How important is this for a Mompreneur?
Finding time to unwind and recharge is IMPERATIVE! If I do not make time for self-care, I slip back in to that dark place of stress and rage and the result is not good for anyone. The critical piece for me is scheduling the time and then keeping that commitment. As women, and Moms, we always put everyone else's needs before our own. When there is an

unexpected event or situation that arises in my day, I typically cut the time from my personal schedule. Even as I am telling this story, I recognize how important it is that I commit to keeping myself as a priority so that I have the energy to fulfill all my roles.

When I do have personal time, I juggle between reading the Bible and praying, working out, spending quality time with Hubby or catching up with my girlfriends. I have learned to be more forgiving when things do not go as planned and appreciate any down time that I do get. On some days, if I can go to the bathroom by myself and take a hot shower for more than 5 minutes, I am winning! When I can get away for a night out with Julio or girls weekend away, I take complete advantage to make up for lost time.

Finding time to unwind and recharge goes back to the whole idea of balance, and sticking to the schedule to make sure personal time happens. This is also where I lean on my Mom and sister to help with the kids so I can get some extra "me" time when needed.

What book would you recommend for a Mompreneur just starting out? Why this particular one?
I was recently introduced to the book <u>Mindset: The New Psychology of Success</u> by Carol S. Dweck. I am participating in an accelerated program, specifically designed for women business owners and we discussed this book early in the program as a foundation to embracing a CEO mindset versus a worker mindset. I was fascinated because not only does this mindset apply to business, but it also impacts how we parent, our education, and other relationships. In brief, it discusses a fixed mindset and a growth mindset. If we can stay in the growth mindset, then we are creating a platform to achieve new levels of growth and success, where the fixed mindset leads to limiting beliefs about what you can achieve. The growth mindset is based on the idea that everything you would ever want or need can be learned. If you want to be better at math for example, you can work really hard, study, and

practice and you can be very successful at math. On the other hand, the fixed mindset would say that you are only good at math if you are born that way. The whole concept has been transformational for me, and I am working to embrace the growth mindset for myself, my family, and my business.

What are some of the ways that you involve or have involved your family in your business?

My husband is way better at involving the kids in our business than me! My version of the kids being involved is chasing them out of my home office daily. They love to sit at my desk and mimic what I do. I have walked upstairs to find Selena sitting at my desk with the phone resting on her shoulder, talking to customers, while typing on the computer and writing on all my papers. She really has me nailed, and she is going to be a great multitasker like Mommy!

On the other hand, Julio lets the kids get hands on with him. Last summer he would rotate taking the older kids with him to work for the day. They would come home with hilarious stories about meeting new customers, helping to install equipment or being their Dad's tool hander and clean up person. The little ones, especially Javi, help Daddy with any and everything possible. We have had several evenings where there are computer brains spread all over the dinner table, and all the kids are gathered around to help him rebuild custom computers. If there is a project where power tools are involved, they are even more engaged and eager. Julio makes almost every situation a comedy show, because that is just his personality. I love it because we complement each other so well. Where I am all about order and structure, he is all about enjoying life and having fun in every moment. His approach to life has helped me to loosen up and life to the fullest.

What did it feel like to make your first dollar as a Mompreneur? How long did that take?

My situation is unique because I joined a business that was already making money, so I started getting paid immediately. The biggest difference in getting paid as an entrepreneur and working for a larger business is the impact of understanding how the cash flows in and out of the business, and the direct impact it has on payroll. When I was in my previous role, I never worried about if I was going to get paid every two weeks. When I made decisions, I had to think like a business owner, but the reality was my pay check was not directly affected. I was paid commissions for hitting targets, so there was incentive to over achieve, but I did not lose money or have the risk of not getting paid if I did not achieve my targets. As an entrepreneur, your money is directly affected by how much money you are bringing in, and how much is going out in expenses. The flow of money is also impacted by contract terms, customers that do not pay on time, and unexpected expenses. I have learned a tremendous amount by managing the finances, and it has absolutely improved my business acumen.

The other piece about being a Mompreneur that no one likes to talk about is that you do not start off with a glamourous salary right away! When the guys agreed to bring me on board, the salary that I was offered was not on par with the industry average, and it was obviously a substantial drop from my previous salary. I understood this from the beginning so I planned accordingly, knowing that my salary would increase as we scaled the business for growth. My purpose and mission outweighed the temporary drop in pay, and I believe and walk in faith that the payoff for growing this business will be far beyond the six-figure salary that I walked away from.

Kids & Significant others, do and say the darndest things. Please share with us one of your funniest moments, embarrassing moments, saddest moments, and most rewarding moment that involving your family and your business?

My kids and husband are absolutely crazy, so let me choose some good examples to give you all some insight in to our lives. My husband, Julio, is known for saying completely random, off the wall, and inappropriate things on a regular basis. It drives me insane most of the time, and all I can do is laugh it off or curse him out. I try my hardest not to do the latter. When I first started working with him, I spent a few days in the field with him so I could gain more insight to his processes and routines. Every customer we met that day, some longtime customers, and some new clients, he told a made-up story about how I begged him to marry me and now I was following him around on jobs. The whole time he is roping the customers in to this story, I am laughing but also beyond embarrassed! Of course, I had to speak up and let them know that is not how the story went down, but I could not control or stop the things that were coming out of his mouth! I saw firsthand how his sense of humor and personality helped him to build relationships with his customers, and break down any barriers that may be in the way of them having an enjoyable experience.

Since I work at home, I have learned to time my customer phone calls for nap time or when the kids are outside playing. I have had more situations than I can count where I am deep in a professional conversation, and my littles come running upstairs yelling "MOMMY!!" My reflexes have improved to hit the mute button with speed, or apologizing when saying that I am working remote for the day. I have never called a company and heard kids in the back ground, so I still make every effort not to let that happen. My office is right at the top of the stairs, and we have a gate that was originally installed to keep them from falling down the stairs, but now it works perfectly to keep them out of my office during the day.

One day, our Nanny was changing the baby, Bella, so the two older littles, Selena and Javi, were playing on the landing area at the top of the steps. I was not on the phone at the time, so I did not mind them sitting there, plus they seemed to be entertained. They caught my attention when I started to hear water hitting the carpet. Before I could finish what I was doing, Selena yelled out, "Javi peed!" I jumped up, and sure enough Javi was practicing his aim by peeing directly on my carpet! The looks on their faces always catch me off guard and soften my reaction. This time, they had this look like they knew it was wrong, but they wanted to laugh so hard. All I could do was hide my smile, and tell them to go down stairs while I took a break to clean up the mess. Only a mompreneur understands the life of cleaning up pee on her break!

One of the most rewarding moments for us happened recently when our oldest daughter, Yazmine, spoke at our church for Father's Day. She was asked to speak about Julio's faith, and how it has impacted her. I helped her prepare leading up to the day, and even the day before she was nervous and was not sure what she was going to say. When she finally stood up there to speak, I do not think there was a dry eye in the house. She did an absolutely beautiful job telling the story of how Julio started his business on a step of faith, how he stepped up as the Father and Mother when their Mom left, and how she never even realized how hard the times were for the family because of how hard Julio worked to support them. His love and strength disguised all of the pain, hurt, and financial struggles that their family was going through. I have heard Julio remind them of how far the family has come, and how blessed we are, but to hear the story from her perspective made my heart so proud and full. The example that Julio has instilled in the kids to go after their dreams, believe that they can overcome any obstacle, and that love is the most important thing in the world is the same thing that reassured me to step out of the security of a corporate job and in to this world as a Mompreneur. I am so thankful for the blessings that God has given me in my husband and kids, and even though I still cannot believe this is my reality, I would not have it any other way. I love them with all of me, and they are the reason that I will never turn back. I am on this journey for a reason, and I will be a Mompreneur for life.

What is Your Favorite Quote?
She is clothed with strength and dignity, she laughs without fear of the future.
Proverbs 31:25

Leave us with ONE word to describe a Mompreneur.
Empowered ~ make (someone) stronger and more confident, especially in controlling their life and claiming their rights.

A Woman's Worth Bio

A few years ago, no one could have convinced Marisa Colón that she would a Mommy to five kids, much less a Mompreneur! In a humorous life transformation, Marisa went from an independent, career focused bachelorette, to a readymade family with her husband and his two children, then a rapid addition of 1, 2, 3 babies back to back. After climbing her way up the corporate ladder, building her brand as a successful leader, and reaching her goal to earn a six-figure salary, Marisa had the picture-perfect life with her beautiful family. She was an inspiration to her team, her peers, and her friends as she pulled of the life of balancing a high demand career while raising a large family.

That was how life looked from the outside. She was a workaholic on the brink of destruction as she struggled to be the mother she never thought she would be. With mounting stress and pressure to be the perfect leader, wife and mother, the ones that she loved suffered the most.

Marisa was introduced to the entrepreneur life when she met her husband, Julio. He was running a security and sub-contracting business with his two brothers, and over the years she saw the business grow and reach new levels of success. While she was out on maternity leave with the baby of the family, she made the hardest decision of her life, and one that would transform her completely. She left the career and team that she loved, and joined forces with her husband and his two brothers to scale their family business to build a legacy for generations to come.

In telling her story, Marisa shares her transformational journey to becoming a Mompreneur with her genuine, straight forward, inspirational touch. Her passion for leading and empowering woman in her career has carried over in to her new life as a Mompreneur, and her story will help women stay grounded in their purpose as they pursue their dreams.

Connect with me:
marisa@mytvs.us
Facebook @Marisa Colón

CHAPTER 7

NADINE DENISE QUARLES

CEO at Coach Niecy Q & Owner/Director at Dream Givers Childcare

Who is the "Mompreneur" behind this business? Tell us about you.

I STARTED MY FIRST BUSINESS in 1998 as a married mother of 3 young girls. I always had a mindset of entrepreneur. When I was younger, I sold Tupperware with my mom. I have Associate's and Bachelor's Degrees in Early Childhood and in June of 2017, I completed my Master's Degree in Business. The degrees encompassed the direction I have for my childcare business.

What made you decide to start the business that you're in?
I decided to start my childcare business because it was birthed in me from my youth. I have always loved babies. I used to line up my baby dolls and tell my mom that I wanted lots of babies, all nationalities; all backgrounds. I started keeping the children in church (I've been a church girl all my life). I went to school and my focus was on business, but I decided to that what I truly wanted to do was to open my own center. I just loved children that much!

My husband and I married when I was 18 and we moved away for 15 years. When we came back home, I started working in a psychiatrist's office. One day I decided I just couldn't do it anymore. I wanted my own business. Honestly speaking, my husband was a little leery at first. He asked if I was sure I wanted to keep kids. My response, "Yes! I love them!"

I started my coaching business in March 2017. As I look back, I have always been drawn to women. When I was in school, my friends would come to me for advice, a shoulder to cry on and someone to talk things out with. I was always willing to help someone through their situation. It seems to have followed me, so I pursued that and went to school for coaching. Today, it is something that I love too!

I love children and women. It's not that I don't love everyone else, but God has given me a heart for children and women of all backgrounds. Now I am a coach for women and have my own daycare center. Dreams do come true.

What made you LEAP? How did you make the leap from a secure paid job to starting your own business?
Let me first say, I have "leaped" several times. My first "leap" was when I moved in 1998 and started by own daycare, for about 6 years. It was a rough road. It wasn't paying much, but I loved what I did. My philosophy

has always been "I have to love the job that I'm on to stay. Money doesn't keep me. Happiness keeps me when it comes to my work."

I talked to my husband because the place I was working was already in the process of laying off. I figured it was time to open my daycare once they laid me off. My husband didn't really like it, but I did it anyway.

The second "leap" occurred when I went back to "work" because I went back to school. I started working at an alternative school. That was a great experience because it taught me so much about children, about people. It taught me how to handle children. It was a challenging job and when I went back into the workforce, it was never a boring day. It didn't matter what I got paid, I was happy all day. It was challenging for me and I always had something new to expect. It gave me so much joy that I actually did that for 5 to 6 years.

Once again it was time to "leap". In 2005, I jumped back into my daycare business. Although the pay was pretty good at the alternative school, my dream was owning my own daycare. Things were going great, and then came the ups and downs of losing children and gaining others. This time, I had so many children that I was overflowing in my home. I went out and rented a building and that went well for a while. Unfortunately, there were some hiccups that sent me back into the workforce. At that time, I began working in someone else's childcare setting while holding down a part time job as well.

My last "leap" was me leaving the childcare facility and beginning again. That's where I am today. I will not "leap" again because I believe that this is my calling and where I am supposed to be. I'm here with my Dream Givers Childcare. That's the "leap of faith" for my childcare.

Let's just get to the Elephant in The Room, how do you balance or how did you balance your work/home life, or is there even such a thing?
For me, I've always been a neat freak; an organizer. I must have things in order. It was tough at first. Having 3 young girls, working my childcare business, going to school to get my associates, having a part time job, and selling Tupperware on the side; there was a lot of juggling! I just had a lot of things in my head. At that time, I just planned everything in my head. I knew I needed to get up, get their hair done, get them off to school, get myself ready, do homework with the kids, homework for my classes, and cook dinner for the family. There were a lot of struggles at times. My husband was great about helping where he could, but he still had to work.

It took time. Over the years I learned how to deal with it. I just jumped and did what I had to do. Sometimes, I missed, sometimes I didn't. I had to put systems in place to get things done. It meant ironing clothes for the week on Saturdays. Meal prep wasn't one of my tools at that time. I would be sitting at work trying to figure out what we would be eating for dinner the next day. My mom did teach me to take my food out early in the morning or the night before. So, the crock pot became my best friend. When I did daycare at home that helped me because I could put my family's meal on for dinner while the kids were napping.

I just kept pushing because I saw the goal ahead and where I wanted to be. As time went on, I became more time conscious, and had more planning and management involved. Of course, we all have "life" to happen and something to go wrong. But we must get back on pace. I find what helps me is a schedule and a plan of action for each day that I get up.

What did you or what do you say to yourself when you feel like giving up?
Back then, looking at my 3 girls, made me say to myself that I can't give up. I had to push for them. I always felt like I couldn't give up because so

many people depended on me. I will be honest. There were times when I would go to the bathroom and cry. But I knew that even if I wanted to quit, I couldn't. My family was depending on me and I had to fight for them.

Giving up is not an option. You can feel like giving, but actually doing it...no can do. I push myself because I know who I am.

What keeps you going?
My children and my desire to help others is what keeps me going. I just enjoy helping others succeed. Whether it's keeping their children, making sure they have a safe place for their child to come while they work, or whether it's giving advice and praying with others, I stay focused on God, realizing that both are a ministry. I can't give up on what God has placed within me. He blessed me with these gifts, so I must keep going until He calls me or He comes back. The gifts that He allowed me to have are what keep me going. I also want to leave an inheritance for my children and family as well as be able to help others. I have a gift of help so that's just who I am.

What was the best advice you ever received? Worst advice?
The best advice I was given was to use my gifts. I should use what was in my hands and use what I have. So many times, we don't use the gifts within us. God has birthed a gift in each one of us.

The worst advice I have received was don't start a business because it's not going to make it. I've probably had plenty nuggets of bad advice, but I try to block those out of my mind.

We all know that saying, "it takes a village to raise a child", but for a mom starting her own business, the village may be a state. So, who do you turn to or go to for help? Who are your go to people/services?
I would first say, because that's just who I am, I go to God in prayer. In the early stages of my childcare business and being a mompreneur, I would go to my mom when I needed a physical person. Within the last couple of years, I've been going to my daughter Jasmine and my

husband Keith. They have become my go to people to bounce ideas off and see where I am going and what I need to get.

What do you do to unwind and recharge? How important is this for a mompreneur?

It is very important for a mompreneur to unwind, recharge, rethink and regroup because you have so much on your plate at times. I go in my office and begin to write, plan and look at my goals, making sure things are on target. To unwind, I clean up and change my desk around. I am a planner, so a lot of my recharging comes through planning. I write things down, make notes, check items off and think of new and creative ways to enhance my businesses. I read my books again from different entrepreneurs and mentors that I have grasped. I get these books out and start regrouping, budgeting and planning. My office is just that place for me to regroup and unwind.

What book would you recommend for a mompreneur just starting out? Why this particular one?

I actually have two books that I would recommend. The first would be "The 9 Steps to Financial Freedom" by Suze Orman. I would recommend it because it will get your finances in order first, before you try to do a business. A lot of times when you try to jump into a business, finances are jacked up and that's just more to handle. I would tell anyone, get your finances in order, find out the steps so you don't have to worry about them and then you can better control your business.

The second book that I would recommend would be "Essentialism: The Disciplined Pursuit of Less" by Greg McKeown. It simply was a good read.

What are some of the ways that you involve or have involved your family in your business?

When I first started my daycare business in 1997, my children were small. As they grew older, I incorporated them as employees. I had name badges for them. My daughter Nicole would be the play teacher, the assistant, the PE teacher and the art teacher. Even today, my family helps me out with both of my businesses, Coach Niecy Q and Dream Givers Childcare. Jasmine works with me and gives me great ideas to incorporate in my business. I'm grateful for that. My husband Keith helps me assist with repairing things when things break down to make sure my business stays up and running. My daughter Tempest has helped me with flyers, memos and things of that nature before I hired a graphic designer.

I am grateful for my family. I incorporated them early. They grew with me and learned the business. One of my daughters is already an entrepreneur of her own. She owns a dance studio. When your children see mom as a mompreneur, some decide that they want to become a mompreneur as well.

What did it feel like to make your first dollar as a mompreneur? How long did it take?

It felt great when the first child came, they made their first payment and I wrote the receipt. It finally felt like this is really real. I could really do it. It took about a month or two once I got my flyers out there and said I was open for business. It took that long to gain one child and it felt awesome to make my own money in my own business. It felt like freedom.

Kids and significant others do and say the darndest things. Please share with us one of the funniest moments, embarrassing moments, saddest moments, and most rewarding moments involving your family and your business?

In my childcare business, one of the most rewarding moments comes when children learn things and you can see what you have taught them from infancy all the way to two or three years old. When one student learned to speak, it just flooded my soul and tears began to roll when I saw her progress.

The saddest moments I guess would be when I first opened in 97 and had to close my childcare. My children were so sad because we had become attached to the kids that I kept. One little boy had been with me for almost three years. We lost contact with him for a while.

One of the funniest moments to my own children, but one of the most embarrassing moments for me was while the childcare students were playing in the back yard. A little boy needed to go to the bathroom, so that's just what he did, right in the yard. My girls laughed so hard, even though I was completely embarrassed.

What is your favorite quote?
"I learned that people will forget what you said, people will forget what you did, but people will never forget how you made them feel."

- Maya Angelou

Leave us with one word that you feel describes a mompreneur.
RESILIENT

Biography for Minister Denise Quarles
Minister Denise Quarles was born and raised in Portsmouth, Virginia. She is the third of six children born to William and Evelyn Perry. After graduating from Manor High School, she was married to Elder Keith Quarles in 1986. From this union, they have been blessed with three beautiful daughters; Tempest, Jasmine and Nicole.

Denise earned an Associate's Degree in Early Childhood Education from Tidewater Community College. She later attended Norfolk State University, where she earned a Bachelor's Degree in Education. In 2007, she earned a Bachelor's Degree in Theology from Holy Light College of Bible. She is currently working on a Masters Degree in Business.

At the age of 13, Denise accepted Jesus Christ as her Lord and Savior. She was baptized and filled with the Holy Spirit, beginning her walk with Christ. Presently, she serves as a minister at New Light Church in

Chesapeake, Virginia under the leadership of Bishop Darryl McClary, Sr. and Pastor Jessica McClary. There, she serves with the Women's Ministry, Media Ministry, the Youth Planning Committee, and is president of the Pastor's Aid Ministry. She is striving daily to live a life that is pleasing to God. It is her heart's desire to see people from all walks of life come to Christ Jesus. One of her favorite scriptures is Hebrews 11:1, "Now faith is the substance of things hoped for, the evidence of things not seen." Building faith, trusting that God will guide her throughout her life and walking in His will, has brought her to where she is today.

Minister Denise Quarles is a powerful preacher and teacher of the Word of God and longs to see the men and women of God walk into their destiny through the Word of God. This desire has led to the launch of "Coach Niecy Q" in October of 2016. As a Life Coach, Denise encourages everyone from entrepreneurs to homemakers to **P.L.A.N. (PREPARE** the plan, **LEAP** into action, **ALIGN** yourself, and **NEVER** stop planning).

In addition to serving as a Life Coach, Denise has been in the childcare industry for over 20 years. She has worked through the ranks as a Teacher Assistant, Teacher, Assistant Director and Center Director. She is now the owner of "Dream Givers Childcare".

Her hobbies include entrepreneurship, shopping and spending time with her family. She has instilled the necessity of a strong family bond in each of her daughters. Because of her desire to expand her work in the Kingdom of God, Denise plans to begin a Women's Ministry Outreach Program.

Social media sites –
Web Page: https://www.coachniecyq.com/
Facebook: https://www.facebook.com/coachniecyq
Instagram: https://www.instagram.com/coachniecyq/

CHAPTER 8

DEIRDRE WILLIAMS-SANDERLIN

Founder & CEO Plan D Global Consulting

Who is the Mompreneur behind the business? Tell us about you.

MY LIFE MAKES THE QUOTE "I AM EVERY WOMAN" come alive! My journey as a solo caretaker of my aging mom (and other extended family members without children); the child/daughter, sister to everyone – you know that it's always that "ONE" that gets the special attention for more reasons than one. I'm that aunt that holds lots of secrets but reprimands from the place only an auntie can. I have been the woman who went from six figure years to no figures, the wife that can bring home the bacon, fry it up in a pan, and never ever let…. you know the rest. I've experienced sudden unemployment; health challenges and just everyday life that has allowed me to become a spokesperson for so many women who have to play the balancing act.

I was born in Norfolk, Virginia but lived much of my very early years of life on the east coast and later returned to Hampton Roads with my mother. I grew up as an only child in a single parent household with lots of extended family support. We have always lived around family; next door, around the corner or in the same home. My mom's support team was a village second to none. I was always traveling, vacationing, staying over or visiting family. Both my parents are first born grandchildren-deeply loved and respected. I was loved even more because I was the first-born grandchild on both sides and because I was their daughter gave me privileges that I now recognize is a rare experience. Though my father was not in the home, I can rarely remember a time that he wasn't around. Though my mom had fantastic support, there is nothing like the experience of growing up in a single parent home. The things that I witnessed my mom contend with made me the fighter that I am today. I just won't give up- I may retreat for a while-but the desire to continue and finish strong is embedded in my mental closet. She is truly the best book I ever witness being written out loud.

I have spent the last 20 years living out my passion working in the Human Serves arena; I even became the Founder and Director of the first Women Center on the campus of one of the largest Historically Black College/University's (HBCU) in the country. I love assisting and motivating women, particularly single moms-encouraging them to look past their current temporary status and dream of who they want to be and who their children could be- just look at me. I survived!

I am now married and the proud POM-MOM of one adorable, stubborn, spoiled, do his own thing Pomeranian, Simba, who has played so many roles in my life. He has been the comforter, the challenger, the rebellious son, my riding partner and a girl's best friend!

What made you decide to start the business that you're in?

Most people are really shocked when I have said, "I really don't know what I want to be when I grow up". While at dinner last year, one of my good friends Jerlaunda, responded- "OH MY GOD DEIRDRE, ARE YOU SERIOUS? I THOUGHT YOU ALWAYS KNEW YOU WERE SUPPOSED TO BE AN EVENT PLANNER". The light bulb came on, I was like- wow, that's what I do and do quite well (lol). Honestly, I have been planning since I was a teenager. From family dinners, surprise parties, family outings to corporate events and now motivational programs for women. I just love the feel of festiveness, impulse and commemoration- just giving someone hopeless complete inspiration. I know that this is one of my natural talents so why not do something that you love, get paid, help people and have a sense of worth and value. To me, it's nothing like feeling that you have facilitated just what someone needed-yep I believe I'll take that job ☺ !

What made you LEAP? How did you make the leap from a secure paid job to starting your own business?

LEAP, Jump or get pushed? I'd like to think that every step, every failure, every success is ordained. Nothing catches God by surprise! I didn't voluntarily LEAP- I had a little help. Actually, funding had run out for the women center that I founded -so my job ended when the funds ended. Many have asked, well why didn't the university continue it- my answer is, "God said, it's time for you to do, Plan-D." And quite frankly, it's the best sabbatical that I could have ever had. Doing something that no one has ever done before and starting from grass roots takes LOTS of energy, time, commitment and sacrifice. My mental and physical faculties really needed a break from being the brainchild and making bricks without straw. Moreover, the same energy that I exhausted in someone else's vision, I could invest in me-at least for this moment. I didn't realize how tired and worn I was until I stopped working. I wholeheartedly believe this was the lesson that I couldn't teach to women anymore, it was the lesson I had to learn- ALWAYS BE PREPARED! This experience ignited the creation of my business Plan-D and has become a platform to teach women how to **S.T.E.P.** (**S**trengthen- Self-Development, **T**ransform, **E**mbrace and **P**repare) even when they feel like their feet just won't move.

How do you balance or how did you balance your work/home life?
Though I believe trying to have balance is something we should go after, I'm not so sure that I really got the whole balancing act down right. I believe in prioritizing; some things I just couldn't do, because home, Simba or work came in first place. Lots of times I couldn't go and participate in other activities, not just because of home, husband or Simba-Bimba, but because I also have to be a support to my elderly mom. I believe women tend to juggle and multi-task more than balancing. I looked up the word balance and some of the words used to describe it was stability, poise and equilibrium. I don't think any of those things describe my life past or present. They don't scream, "That's Deirdre". I just do the best I can do from minute to minute to make sure that there is some normalcy and that most days I get it right; not perfect, but improving.

What do you say to yourself when you feel like giving up? What keeps you going?
One thing I pride myself on is my genuineness -if I can just be real for just a moment. Many like to sugar coat their experiences and reactions to their experiences. The truth is, sometimes you really tick your own-self off sometimes, wouldn't you agree? After you have poured ALL of you out to everything and everybody else, sometimes you just feel like you don't have any left for you. There are a lot of things I say and do to

maintain my sanity when I feel like giving up. Now, I just told you that I like to keep it real, so try not to judge me too harshly. I began by having a very transparent conversation with myself by asking myself questions, and yes, I'm not the norm, I answer (lol). The questions begin at, "Now what is going on with you now Deirdre"? "Why are you going through this" and sometimes "Why are you going through this again?" I may even say a few choice four letter words (told you don't judge me, I'm only human). **After I have cross examine every particle and tissue in my body, the light bulb comes on and I recognize that, I got this! So I** move to my affirmations- I AM, I WILL and I MUST. Reminiscing and rehearsing my goals, my dreams and GOD's promises really keep me going.

What was the best advice you ever received? Worst advice?

Throughout the years, people have suggested and made recommendations on what they thought I should and shouldn't do. Sometimes I listen; most times I did it my way, more times than not, I should have listened. I remember years ago an extended family member told my mother, that I wasn't college material. Oh my goodness that hurt me to my core-but the comment detonated my inner will to complete what I had started. The best thing that anyone could have said to me was, "YOU CAN DO AND BE ANYTHING YOU WANT TO BE, ALL YOU HAVE TO DO IS START MOVING"! Of course, I know there were some more ingredients to just moving-but that was the first step- Faith without works is DEAD! Needless to say, I have a few letters behind my name now that illuminates the message of the Greatest Best Seller and answers the questions to many and even myself if I was capable, noteworthy or even qualified for this journey- the word says "For I KNOW THE PLANS I HAVE FOR YOU declares the LORD, plans to PROSPER you and not to harm you, plans to give YOU HOPE and a FUTURE", Jeremiah 29:11. And guess what? I believe it! I am fertile ground and I am looking forward to all that God will birth through me.

We All know the saying It takes a village to raise a child, but for a mom starting her own business, the village may be a state. So who do you turn to or go to for help? Who are your go-to people/services?

The old African Proverb rings boldly in my soul, especially being from a two-person household that work traditional 9-5's and run two businesses. With that amount of commitment, things sometime go lacking or feels like it's not getting everything it or they need. My story is slightly different than most, because it is my Pomeranian that benefits immensely from a village that goes over and beyond to help me with my fur-baby Simba. They give me so much peace when I have to be away for long periods-they are just an awesome group of people! My village is made up of a host of relatives, neighbors and close friends. They are people that will get up in the wee hours of the night to take care of Simba for me just like he is one of their own children. They pick him up for me, dog sit when I have to I work late, come over and walk him and even become Simba's home away from home when we vacation. This village of nanas, aunties, cousins and dog-friends is the absolute best; they have made my transition into Pom-hood very easy. Particularly since Simba's is not a human baby his communication style is not the traditional way of conversing- he has a special way to let you know that he is hungry, sick, happy, or sad. He doesn't have the ability to let himself out to go potty or go in the kitchen and make a sandwich or call grandma on the telephone. That means when we have to leave him, we have to make sure that it is with someone that truly understands that and is willing to watch him like he is their own. Very similar to most moms, you just don't leave your children with anybody. It has to be someone that you trust wholeheartedly. In recent months, we had an unexpected tragedy in my family. My dear nephew Jesse was murdered. That was just an awful time. We had to make travel plans and where was I going to leave him? Everyone in my village was going on the same road trip. I was just an emotional mess- the dog sitters were booked. The doggy motels needed a weeks' notice and I didn't have that notice to give. Luckily, one of the Cheering Coaches called me and said "I know you didn't leave my baby at home by himself". Mind you, we were on the road and my sister-in-law had come over to let him out for his morning walk. But just to hear her say that, made my heart go pitter-patter! Needless to say, Simba jumped into the car with his auntie and stayed with his God-mommy J. The relief that that intervention and support gave was priceless! Just because I'm a Pom-Mom doesn't mean that I don't have the same trepidation that most moms feel when leaving their children with caretakers. It's just as scary…I probably worry just as much.

What do you do to unwind and recharge? How important is this for a Mompreneur?

No matter if you are a mompreneur or just a mom and the CEO of your home, it is essential that you learn how to unwind and recharge. You have got to step away and retreat from all of the many hands and urgencies that pull at you daily. All of the stressors can cause the **mom** and the **preneur** to CRASH! I use to get so overwhelmed because I was like an Octopus with eight arms in EVERYTHING. So now I've learned how to stay in my lane, limit my "I AM EVERY WOMAN" take over spirit, and take a scheduled time each week to just release and retreat. I color, I read, I meditate or I call one of my friends and laugh, laugh and laugh some more until my body is literally light again.

What book would you recommend for a Mompreneur just starting out? Why this particular one?

Everyone needs a map and a mentor (physical or conceptual). Stepping out to become an entrepreneur is very scary and many women, particularly mompreneurs don't have a support system. Some of them are likely to have been stay at home moms and off of the social grids for a while and may not really know where to go to find solid approaches to run effective businesses. If I were to recommend a book for Mompreneurs, it would be "Make the Day Count" by John Maxwell. The book gives you clear instructions about how to make your daily agenda effective and productive. The tools that the author shares are practical strategies that are relatable and easy to implement into the busy woman's schedule.

What are some of the ways that you involve or have involved your family in your business?

My family has always been involved in my business. Most of them were guinea pigs that I used for trial and error. They have been to all my parties, participated in all the girl talks, round table discussions, set up tables for events, made centerpieces, marched in the parades, recruited key note speakers, sung, danced, played musical instruments, and facilitated forums. Yes, they have done it all! Family is everything-they will be the best-committed critique you'll ever have. They are woven in my blanket of success. They have been my acoustic motivation in every step I've taken.

What did it feel like to make your first dollar as a Mompreneur? How long did that take?

When I got my first check written to Plan D Global Events, it was the most thrilling, humble experience I have ever had. It was like a scene from the movie Gladiator- at that moment, I recognized I had come full circle. .

One of my most rewarding moments was being able to host a women's conference one year after my job ended and have a sold-out crowd. This was the evidence, the motivation, the validation that I needed to know that this was truly my calling and that I could have been doing this all the time. The highlight was that my elderly mom was there to witness it!

Being an entrepreneur is one of the hardest jobs that you will ever have. I don't know if there is just one thing or a group of things that just broke my heart other than the inconsistency of funding. Admittedly, there have been lots of sad moments, perhaps more than happy ones.

The more no's than yes's, the long hours, the investment with no immediate return, the time that you are away from your family, the missed vacations-yet I still take great strength in knowing that delay is not denial.

One of embarrassing moments was a few years ago when my husband and I had gone out of town on business and had to leave Simba with his temporary foster mom. As most parents do, I called several times a day to check on Simba and his foster mom related that, he is just fine. On the third day, I called and didn't get any answer and no return call. Late that night, I began to worry and called her husband's phone, she answered and shared the news that made my heart drop. Simba got out of her gate and ran up to a pit-bull. Yes, sigh- I was numb! She stated that her roommate was in the yard and left the gate open and another neighbor was walking his dog and Simba ran after them. I was in tears-I just knew Simba was dead then she said, calm down, Simba is fine; he is just a little shaken, the Pit just slapped him around. Needless to say, the business trip was cut short and we returned to Hampton Roads the following day. Well, my husband decides to go and interview the entire neighborhood to see who owned the pit bull. People were calling and texting me saying, De, your husband is out in the neighborhood knocking on doors looking for some Pitbull owner. Lord, really? I was so embarrassed! I asked him, what are you going to do, beat the Pitbull up? Ask for his side of the story? Oddly enough he knocked on enough doors to find the Pitbull owner. He mean mugged the Pit and left, lol.

After we decided to adopt Simba, we had to get him acclimated to our busy lifestyles. So many mornings I would be rushing out the door to give him a quick walk and make it to appointments. This particular morning was no different. I was on skates going out the door to take Simba to the track for our morning walk- so I put Simba in the car and realized I had left my phone in the house. I went back in the house to get the phone as my neighbor was pulling up in his driveway. Our neighbors owned a nearby restaurant. Simba would often greet them by running across the yard with his passionate barking. After I got my phone, I came back to get in the car and I didn't see Simba. Now to give you a little history. Simba was very new to us and to our families-Simba wasn't familiar with them and he would put on a barking marathon until they left. It became a running joke that someone was going to put Simba on a hotdog bun and he would be a filling lunch for somebody on the go. My neighbor was coming back out of his house; Simba wasn't barking and nowhere to be seen. I panicked and ran to him and asked quite elevated, "Did you see my dog"? He said your dog? I said yes Simba? He said, I haven't seen your dog-well, the female hormones were kicking and I just lost it; I have no idea what I said, was frantic-screaming at my neighbor... "You know what dog, he barks at you every day; he was in my car"! My neighbor said, "I haven't seen your dog." My neighbor started walking me out of his walkway towards my car- I looked in the car and the tears begin to roll, open the car door and the dog was up in the back window like a cat, looking at me like "this chic is plum crazy, but she is one cool ride or die"! His coat is the same color of my car interior and he just blended in. It was absolute hilarious story to tell my family that I thought that someone had made Simba out of a Hotdog, but I have never felt so small accusing someone so unfairly. I learned some valuable business tips from that one encounter:

* Research is essential to become an effective business leader
* If you don't see it the first time, go back and review it again.
* Study your craft, one quick look, and you could miss something very valuable.
* Never give up looking for something that you love
* Things are not always as they seem, they may look alike, have the same color or characteristics but may end up being nothing like you expected

What is Your Favorite Quote?
Nothing is Impossible the word itself spells IM Possible! A. Hepbern

Leave us with ONE word to describe a Mompreneur.
Resilient

A Woman's Worth Bio
Deirdre W. Sanderlin is the CEO of Plan-D, "The Wonder Woman Emissary" where women are transformed by way of her unique traveling women's center. Deirdre is noted for her creative and non-traditional strategies to provide relevant programming that address the many needs of young girls and women. Her commitment and passion to assist women in reaching their full potential and personal platform is second to none; teaching women how to **S** trenghten self-development **T** rans-form **E** mbrace and **P** repare is her heart's desire. DEIRDRE credits all of her bravery to God and to her tenacious mom, Rita Williams. She is known as a master motivator and an unapologetic believer in Christ she lives by the motto, nothing is impossible, the word itself spells I'M POSSIBLE.

She Thought She Could, So She Did- SO CAN YOU!

PlanD Global Events
4540 Princess Anne Road, Suite 114
Virginia Beach, Va. 23462
757.354.1234

CHAPTER 9

PATRICIA LAURENCEAU JEAN-LOUIS

CEO At Rebrand To Profit

Who is the "Mompreneur" behind this business? Tell us about you.

I AM PATRICIA LAURENCEAU JEAN-LOUIS your ReBrandologist. My mission is to help women entrepreneurs do three things in their business. The first is to gain clarity, so you clearly understand your "Why" and know who you were called to reach. The second is increase visibility so the ones you were called to reach know that you even exists and know what you do. The third is to expand your reach so you can connect with a larger pool of individuals within your target audience resulting in increased profits. My mission is to add greater value and provide the tools necessary to take your brand to the next level. My focus is to empower you with the strategies you need to build a brand that is **AMAZINGLY** successful. It does, however, require lots of hard work, but I am here with you every step of the way as you go through your journey.

You are meant to do **GREAT** things. Your life is much more than having the "Monday Blues" and "Thanking God, It's finally Friday." **If you're stuck at a job that you hate only to look forward to payday, life will continue to pass you by as you go around this same mountain.** If you've started the business that you love but it looks more like an expensive hobby because it's not making any money, it will probably get worse without the right information.

That's why I created **ReBrand to Profit**. I created it for women entrepreneurs who are looking for the tools to making it happen in their business, their brand and their life. You know the brand message that you want to convey but don't quite know how to convey that brand message effectively to your audience. I provide information focused on discovering, building and turning your brand into a profitable business.

I am also founder of Kickstart Your Brand Podcast which is a weekly podcast that provides the tips, information and strategies for building a successful brand. Understanding that every problem has a solution, and that every question has an answer, when given proper information you're able to make more informed decisions and develop the business that is right for you. Making informed decisions about your business allows you to save time, money and energy while growing your business, your brand and your life more efficiently and successfully. Kickstart Your Brand Podcast was created to do just that.

Your business is meant to succeed. You are meant to make a significant impact and make a meaningful difference in the world. With each year that passes by, you're getting older while your list of New Year's resolutions keeps repeating itself. So, what are you waiting for? What is holding you back? What is really keeping you from pursuing the purpose that you were destined for? My job is to help women entrepreneurs declutter all that emotional baggage, get rid of your fears, soar above self-doubt, and do away with procrastination once and for all and build the business, the brand and the life you want and dreamed of.

What made you decide to start the business that you're in?
I actually did not choose the business that I am in today. My journey has been a living example of Psalms 37:23 being demonstrated in my life. Psalms 37:23 KJV reads; *"The steps of a good man are ordered by the Lord: and he delighteth in his way."* Branding and marketing was nowhere in sight as a possible career or business that I would ever get into. My desire since I was four years old was to be in business. I knew I would be a boss, have employees and lead people. I was just not clear in what. That part I didn't quite figure out. I spent years trying different businesses and selling all kinds of products trying to find the thing that I was supposed to be doing. Before getting into the graphic/web design industry I first started a gift basket business. I have to admit that I never really saw myself as being a creative individual at all. I started this business because I wanted to fill a niche in the market and this business allowed to me engage with other business and develop business relationships with in my community. I knew going in if I was going to do this I couldn't play

small. My objective was to pursue corporate clients. I watched similar gift basket businesses pursue individual customers for birthdays and holidays which was the norm. I knew I had to stand out and I had to go big and get corporate contracts instead of individual customers. In doing so I began to exercise my creative muscles which at the time was lacking. I didn't know much about the industry but I was willing to learn and learn fast. In the process, I realized that the key to my success was how I marketed my business and brought awareness to what I had and present it to the right corporate clients. My only issue, as most small businesses have in the early stages of their business, is a solid marketing budget. Needless to say, by marketing budget was very slim. It was actually more like none. Like most small business I decided to take on the challenge of creating my own marketing materials. The only problem with that brilliant idea was that I didn't know how to create marketing materials myself. I had no design skills; I had no photos of the baskets that I was creating, and no money to pay someone to do it for me. But I was not about to give up yet. I decided to take a Photoshop course at one of the local community colleges here in Miami. I will never forget this 6 week course which cost me $180 and absolutely changed the trajectory of my life forever. This one course gave me the fundamentals of design that I needed. I remember after the course was over I would sit in front of my computer for hours learning and perfecting different skills. I started creating my own marketing materials which helped me grow my gift basket business. The amazing thing was that as I was getting my marketing materials out people were reaching out to me, not to order baskets, but to find out who was creating my materials for me. Now I started building design clients while working my gift basket business. This is why I say the business chose me. It was never my plan or my intention it was simply divine order operating in my life. I take no credit because all I did was follow the leading of the Lord in my life. The plan I had for my life was to go to law school. I always saw myself as being very analytical. I'm a thinker, I love organization, and administration is my strong suit. So being a carefree creative individual is not how I would have ever described myself. But clearly that's how God did. So, I knew getting into this industry wasn't something that was of me but was definitely something that was given to me as a gift from God.

What made you LEAP? How did you make the leap from a secure paid job to starting your own business?

By nature, I'm a risk-taker. I love change; I love trying new things; I love inquiring about things that I'm not familiar with. So, by nature I'm very comfortable in that zone. When it came to take that LEAP into the entrepreneurial pool it has always been something that I wanted to do. My only question was how was I going to make this happen? Being an entrepreneur has always been a part of my DNA from the age of 4. Even at that age I knew I would have my own business. The only question I had at the time was in what industry. When the

time finally came for me to take that leap of faith, I can honestly say it was at the worst time ever. Being single with no children would have been the optimal opportunity and time for me to take that risk because then my responsibility and my focus was just on me. Instead I continued to grow as an entrepreneur, build business relationships, further developed my skills as a designer and became more grounded in my purpose. While all of this was going on professionally, life started happening personally. Now I'm married, still running my gift basket business on the side, in addition to building my design clients while working a full-time very stressful job. As if that wasn't quite a bit to juggle I get pregnant with my daughter after being married 5 months. At this point I am starting to feel the stress and overwhelm beginning to creep in. I'm one that loves change but it was so much happening all at the same time. At this point I decide to give up the gift basket business and only working with my design clients but that was still difficult to manage. All the preparation I did never prepared me for all the curve balls that life was throwing me. How in the world was I supposed to keep all these balls in the air? Once again, I get another curve ball. This time I am pregnant with my son. During this time, I was working my design client but not as diligent as I was in the beginning. I was still trying to figure out being and entrepreneur with working full time, a wife and new mom the two babies. I remember being home with my son and making the decision that I did not want to go back to my nine-to-five anymore. For me and all that was going on in my life I could not work my business on the side and work a 9 to 5. It had to be one or the other. I at the time was working as an office manager for a law firm here in Miami and the attorney that I work for was a high-profile attorney who handled some major cases so it is not only a busy office but it was very stressful. I remember days going to work just stressed because of the amount of responsibilities that I had on my job. Around the same time my dad was preparing to retire after 33 years with his company. He was so proud of his accomplishment and the honor he received from the company that he dedicated his years of service to. At his retirement ceremony, they gave him a pin, a plaque and a video recorder as his gifts. He bought his retirement home in Florida to enjoy the remainder of his years. My dad fulfilled his purpose and lived the life he intended to live. His generation believed in staying and committing to your work until the end. And he did just that. For me I wanted to do more. I wanted to leave more behind. So, working for a company for 33 years was not part of the plan for me. When you have children and a family of your own you begin to think of how you will define the concept of legacy for you. This was the first time I waivered and questioned my decision because now I had responsibilities and my decision would not just affect me but will affect them as well. I can take the blows but as a mom we never want our children to feel the impact. Here I was making the decision to go from a two-income household to a one-income household so it was one of those decisions that I could not make lightly but I knew that God was there guiding me through the process. I can't say that it was easy but I can say that it was totally worth it because I am in my purpose. If I had the opportunity to do it again I would do it the exact same way because now looking back 6 years later I realize that I so much resilience, so much determination, and so much fight that was in me. In the process God allowed it to be pulled out of me. It was that resilience, that determination and the fight that I drew from to take the LEAP and keep on going.

How do you balance or how did you balance your work/home life?

As we continue to evolve in an information age we realize that the landscape of corporate jobs is not what they used to be. Being a mompreneur has certainly changed how we view ways of earning an income to support your family. The notion of work-life balance is often the thing that I have grappled with in pursuit of fulfilling my purpose and having an amazing family. As a mompreneur it is a lot of pressure when, often, it is suggested the importance of being able to balance making time for a growing family at home and building a career. It is suggested that being able to accomplish both is key in reaching a level of success. When you are not able to do that well you feel the pressures of society and wonder is it even possible. So, for me the question has always been how do I obtain work-life balance and is it even possible? I don't think it's a one size fit all answer. I've learned that you must be able to create a work-life balance that works for you, your family and your business. The reality is that it may not look like what is working for another mompreneur. For me, I had to get out of the mold of making my work-life balance look like what was working for someone else. The truth is my family is different, my purpose is different and my business is different. So, I had to develop a balance that worked for me. It was not an overnight process. It took trial and error and it took time to get it right for you. Keep in mind that as your family grows, your relationship with your husband matures, your business begins to flourish you must leave room to consistently manage and adjust your work-life balance. I had to evaluate the things that were important to me at the time and focus on those areas until the time came to adjust. When I was single I was attending networking event 3 to 4 times a week. I believed in building connections, and developing relationships to grow your business effectively. But now it is clearly not possible and that's O.K. I had to be fine with missing some networking events so I could attend my daughter's school play. I could not be as accessible to clients after hours because my children and husband needed my attention. What was most important to me in this journey of work-life balance was enjoying the process while understanding that everything was not going to be perfect all of time. For me work-life balance may mean that the kids may go to bed without a shower because I'm just too tired to deal with that ordeal. It may even mean that everyone is eating a peanut butter and jelly sandwiches for dinner because I simply don't feel like cooking. Ultimately, you must determine what works for you and what success looks like for you. Everyone's definition of success is different. For me being able to take my children to school in the morning, being able to pick them up in the afternoon and hear about what happened that day in school, and rushing them to practice after school is success for me. Having the ability to meet with my girlfriend for lunch on a Wednesday after is success for me. It is also being able to take a vacation without having to ask my boss if I can take the time off. Now, I can plan it according to what works for me and my family. Don't get me wrong, the money is important because you must take care of your family. There are certain things that you must place in order for you to live but I think a lot of times we put so much emphasis on material things. I believe that achieving work-life balance is doing the things that are important to you.

What do you say to yourself when you feel like giving up? What keeps you going?

This journey has not been an easy journey but I must say it has been so well worth it. I have discovered so much about myself in the process that is far beyond simply starting, running and growing a business. It has pulled things out of me that I did not even know where in me. I developed a greater sense of resilience, determination, fight and commitment. It was very easy for me to give up on things when it got difficult and move on to something else. But when you have found the thing that you were created to do you stick to it until you fulfill your purpose. So regardless to how difficult the road gets you stay on it because you know this road was designed with you in mind and the road block that you may encounter on the journey you will over ride. There were plenty of times I wanted to give up because it got difficult. I got to points in by business where I simply wanted to throw in the towel and go back to working a 9 to 5 because at least I knew that at the end of the week I would get a check. But it was in those moments where a still quiet voice would remind me to keep moving and don't stop. I would always keep in mind the alternative to quitting my business which was going back to a 9 to 5, not have the flexibility on taking vacations and time off when I wanted, hating the job because I knew I had a greater purpose than working for someone. The thought of that made me sick to my stomach. I know what I've been created to do so every time I wanted to give up I would just think of the alternative, pull myself back up again, get the courage and the energy to say you know what keep it going. There were days that I literally had to stand in front of the mirror and say, "You know what you are you were created to be." "You are an entrepreneur, you are amazing, and you are a multi-millionaire. "You are able to speak into the lives of women and change the course of how they think and see themselves that is an amazing gift." I had to keep reminding myself that I was not doing this for me but for the entrepreneurs that I was called to reach. I'm a natural encourager and an optimist by nature. I love to encourage and see the bright side of things. But sometimes it's easier to encourage someone else than it is to encourage especially, when you find yourself in the darkest moments in your business. However, what I have found was that in those moments God has a way of reminding you of what is on the inside of you. He will remind you of who He called you to be and what your purpose is. I would always remember seeing myself as a little girl running my first business from our bathroom, having my sister as my employee at the age of 4. Before working in my business full-time and quitting my job there was always a feeling of unsettling that I had. I always felt out of place as if I just didn't belong. No matter what job I had or how much I was paid there was always this feeling of unsettling because that wasn't where I needed to be. But it was that still small voice and encouraging myself that kept me going.

What was the best advice you ever received? Worst advice?
The best advice I had ever received was from Marie Forleo several years ago. I enrolled in her program B School and I don't even remember how I even came across her. I remember it was right after I had resigned from my job and I was home on the computer and I saw her program. I looked into it and knew I had to join her program. In one of her she said that everything is "figureoutable." This was a phase that she coined. Simply put according to Marie, every problem had a solution and all it took was your willingness to figure it out. When clearly understood that concept it changed how I saw my life, how I did things, and how I perceived problems. Oftentimes we make problems in our lives much bigger than what it really is. But if you understand that there's a solution to every problem you then look at a problem as a situation that you have the ability to find an answer to.

The worst advice I've ever gotten was during the darkest moments in my business. I had a friend tell me that maybe I was not cut out to be an entrepreneur and maybe I should consider getting a real job. One thing I've learned is that you never make a life altering decision on a temporary situation. I am so glad I did not listen to that advice.

We All know the saying It takes a village to raise a child, but for a mom starting her own business, the village may be a state. So who do you turn to or go to for help? Who are your go-to people/services?
It certainly takes a village especially as a mompreneur to start a business while having a family. As an entrepreneur, you don't know everything

and you can't be afraid to ask for help. Like a new mom you need help when you are raising children. You rely on friends, family, etc. for the best advice when it comes to your children. It's the same thing with a business. You need help from people who are much further than you are and are where you want to be. I have a mentor that I go to for business advice and I rely on when I get stuck. When you are a creative entrepreneur you have so much vision, ideas and concepts that you want to start working on at times all at the same time. But you often need someone that will keep you on track, help you make sense of all of your ideas and suggest the one that you should implement now and put on the shelf to revisit later. What I have found that being around like-minded individuals also helped me grow as an entrepreneur. As I grew my business I had to turn to family especially when it came to get help with the kids when I had an event to attend. Sometimes even as an entrepreneur we're so focused on the area that we're most gifted in. We focus more on our craft and developing that not realizing that we need help in other areas. For me I spent countless hours perfecting my skills in design and developing my skills in web development. The down side to that was the areas that I didn't like was being neglected. For those areas like email marketing, handling my books, managing client projects I had to hire help for. There was no way I could continue being effective in my business and not hire help as I was growing. My go to services are Fiverr, Legal Zoom, UpWork, and Creative Market. These are so many others that I use as well but these are my main ones.

What do you do to unwind and recharge? How important is this for a Mompreneur?

It took some time for me to understand the importance of unwinding and recharging as a mompreneur. I literally reached the point of burn out and overwhelm before I realized that I really needed time off of work and some time to myself. I went from being single to married, having two children, quitting my 9 to 5, and running my business full-time all in the matter of 3 years. Everything was happening so quickly at times I felt like I was in a whirlwind. I was constantly going and going with no break and no time to myself. There were nights my husband would come home from work and I'll be knocked out just exhausted from dealing with the kids, working on my business and doing the things that kept my house functioning, like laundry, grocery shopping, cleaning and cooking. I remember having a conversation with a friend of mine and I was telling her I was feeling so overwhelmed to the point that I felt like I was spinning my wheels and not really going any-

where. As a mompreneur we have so much on our plate and we do so much on a daily basis. We are working to keep our clients happy with us, we are trying to please our husbands, be there for our children and be a great friend to our girlfriend. In the process, we put ourselves last. We don't pay attention to our own emotional state until we are at the point of losing our marbles. I realized that I had to reverse that order and take care of myself. For me to be physically and emotionally available to all those that was pulling from me I needed to first be available to myself. For me what was very important was having a schedule. My rule was if it wasn't on the calendar it was not getting done. No exceptions. The reason I had to do that was because being a mompreneur especially if you are working from a home office your friends and family really don't understand that you really work and you're not home during the day watching television. Time management is a key to the successful operation of your business and your day. The silly phone calls during the day to discuss the family drama with your sister will end up making you frustrated and annoyed and result in an unproductive day. I could not afford that. I had to account for my time because it affected my bottom line. I routinely woke up at 5:30 am daily. This was my time to pray to God and time to me before the chaos started in my house. That was important for me to keep my sanity. Keeping a schedule for the kids was so very important as well. It eliminated conflicts in my schedule with clients and frustration for me. Once the kids were in daycare it made things easier for me and helped to get them on a routine as well. I would drop them off at daycare around 8 am, I would start work at 8:30 and end at 4 pm and pick them up by 4:30 pm daily. I also made it a rule that I did not take any client calls or respond to emails after 4 pm. That allowed me to set some boundaries with clients and focus my attention on the kids and my husband when we got home. By 8:00 pm or 8:30 pm they're in the bed and that is my time to unwind and relax before bed. A schedule makes thing flow so much better for me. I would not be able to survive if I did not keep a schedule. I would not be able to survive if my kids were going to bed at whatever time they wanted. For me something as simple as just watching a funny movie or a show that I found was hilarious help me to unwind. In addition, I made a conscious decision to take more girls trips. I love taking trips with the family however we are still working as moms when we are away with the kids. You still must make sure the kids eat, get them dressed, and do daughters hair, which is a job of its own. When you are on a girl's trip you are focused on just you. No kids, no husband, no house and no work, simply you. That is the best way to unwind in my opinion.

What book would you recommend for a Mompreneur just starting out? Why this particular one?

My all-time favorite book is "Start with Why": How Great Leaders Inspired Everyone to Take Action by Simon Sinek. It is an amazing book and I recommend it to any entrepreneur starting or thinking about starting a business. This book really inspired me to do the work and live a life that inspires me every day. Often, we do or live the lives that others think we should live. Though I knew at a very early age that I was going to be an entrepreneur when I was getting ready to graduate high school I had in my mind that I was doing to go to college and major in political science with a goal in mind of eventually going to law school to become an attorney. That dream was what my parents had for me. Not anything that I had for myself. But what I had to understand and clearly articulate was "WHY" graphic design, web development, branding the thing I was supposed to be doing. The answer to that question had to be more than money or profit. The answer had to be the thing that inspires me daily and the people I serve daily. As a branding and marketing consultant I share with clients all the time that as a brand we're created to solve a problem for a specific group of individuals. Our job is to find out whom we were called to reach and how do we inspire them in a way that encourages them to live their best life and inspire others. Each story forces you to see your life and your business from a totally new perspective. You learn that when you start with "WHY" it is the driving force behind what you do and why you do it. When you want to give up it's the "WHY" that keeps you pushing forward. Despite what the situation may look like, because you understand and you know that there is a greater purpose behind what it is that you're doing as an entrepreneur you keep moving. Sometimes it's a crawl, a stroll or even a slow pace but the point is that you keep moving and eventually you start running again. As a mompreneur there is a leader in you that others are waiting for to inspire them to take action

What are some of the ways that you involve or have involved your family in your business?
Being a mompreneur is not an easy job and to do it well you need help. For me I've had to look to family for help in my business. I was very fortune to have nieces that were much older than my children that were without question my backbone when I needed help with the kids because I had a speaking engagement, or business event to attend. I really attribute much of my success to them because I would not have been able to do it without their help.

I learned years ago from Bishop T.D. Jakes when he was giving advice to leaders in building a strong team, he said, "be slow to hire and quick to fire". That is a piece of advice that has been with me as

I continue to grow my business. When it comes to family I've learned that you have to be really slow to hire because if it doesn't work out it will not only affect your working relationship but will also affect your personal relationship. I do however involve my husband and my children in my business in some aspect. When I do speaking engagements, I want the kids to be there to see what mommy does so they have an understanding of what it is that I do in the lives of other people. I want them to understand that my voice impacts and inspires the lives of so many people. I believe with children the best way for them to learn and understand what you do is to watch you in action. So in being consistent with how I function on a daily basis teaches them the importance of having a good solid work ethic and being available to serve others in your business which is very important. I do take the kids with me at different events that allow children again to set them in a different environment to understand what I do. Let me just say that it doesn't always turnout the way I want with my two because they have minds of their own. The pre-disclaimers I give them both in the car on the way to an event about what my expectations of them are always goes out the window the minute they get out of the car. However my prayer is that when they get older it will make a difference without killing me first.

What did it feel like to make your first dollar as a Mompreneur? How long did that take?

I will never forget making my first dollar as a mompreneur it was the best day ever. I had just resigned from my full-time job while on maternity leave and knew that I had one more check coming in the mail. It was actually my first week working from home. I had a client that had inquired about my web design services the month before and I had not heard back from her. While home working she called and was ready to start her web design project immediately and wanted to know how to make her payment. I was absolutely blown away and ecstatic at the same time. For me it just confirmed that I was doing the right thing and that I had to keep on going.

Kids & Significant others, do and say the darndest things. Please share with us one of your funniest moments, embarrassing moments, saddest moments, and most rewarding moment that involving your family and your business?

My kids are both funny and embarrassing. You can always count on them to make their presence known where ever we go. Sometimes I would prefer no one even know that we are in the room but trust me when I say it will not take long before others know that we are there, it really doesn't. I remember going to a book reading for a friend of mine who had launched her first children's book. Since it was for a children's book it was expected that there would be children there. So of course I'm bringing the kids. On the way there I do what I always do in the car is give me infamous speech to the kids. First off, they both look at me and start reciting what they have already heard me say 100 times before. The rule is no touching, no yelling, no running and stay next to mommy at all times. Where ever mommy goes you go. So clearly they already know the drill. But guess what happens when we walk in? They both act like they never heard a thing. The event was being held at a restaurant. So as soon as we walk in my son takes off running through the restaurant because he sees balloons clear across the dining room. My daughter heads straight to the buffet line because she call herself a foody and if there is food she is there. I am left standing at the entrance of this restaurant thinking to myself I am going to kill these two when I get my hands on them. Half way through the restaurant the author walks towards me with my son in hand and ask me if he was mine. Well, in that moment I wanted to decline, but my son burst out, mommy, where were you? I was looking for you? I thought you left me. I should have left him. He took off running as soon as he walked in the restaurant and he left me but what kind of mother do I look like arguing with a 4-year-old in front of the author. My daughter was already picking out what she wanted on the buffet line because according to her she had to rush to the line because she noticed it was only one red velvet cake left. What??? What about the conversation we had in the car? All I can say is that they both have minds of their own and clearly, I am simply here to go along with their shenanigans.

The saddest and yet the most rewarding moment involving my family and my business is recently being a care giver to my father who is in the early stages of Alzheimer's and Dementia. My dad had a stroke back in April 2016 which caused him to go from a hospital to rehab for 6 weeks. He was beginning to show signs of some improvement but I quickly realized that the father I once knew was no longer. Upon being discharged from rehab my dad had to have 24-hour care. It was really tough on me because with the chaos of being a mom, wife, and entrepreneur now I was faced with making the decision to be a care giver to my dad and move him in my home to care for him. This was a rewarding opportunity because my mom died of asthma when I was 13 years old. I watched her suffer with asthma and go in and out of the hospital when she had an attack but I never had the opportunity to care for her. With my dad, I felt that I was given the opportunity to do so for him. My dad was a single dad raising three kids on his own and I don't know many men today that would do what my dad did. Of course, like everything else in my life it is never at the right time. How am I going to juggle this in addition to everything else I have going on? I love my dad and I want what is best for him but how do I do this with a husband, two small children and a business that requires so much of my attention. My answer, you do it only by the grace of God. Keep in mind I am not dealing with the man that loved me, took care of me, and provided for me. I am now dealing with a man that could not put his thoughts together to express how he's feeling. I am dealing with a man that easily gets disoriented when trying to find the bathroom for the hundredth time. I'm dealing with a man who doesn't realize he is hungry and his lunch becomes dinner. I am dealing with a man that can't remember what day of the week it is but can tell me how his day was at work even though he has been retired for nearly 10 years. It's sad because watching your parent go through this is tough and there is nothing you can do. It's tough because he is declining so quickly. But it is rewarding because I have been given this opportunity at God has placed some amazing people in my life to help me in the process. It is also rewarding because despite the fact that there is a lot that he can't remember and a lot that he is confused about he still remembers who I am and he reminds me of the love he has for me. For that I am truly grateful.

What is your favorite quote?

My favorite scripture is Ephesians 3:20 which read, *"Now unto him that is able to do exceedingly abundantly above all that I can ask or think according to the power that lies within me."* I love that scripture because it is conditional. According to the scripture I have the ability to determine how exceedingly and abundantly God can operate in my life because his measure is determined by the limitations that we remove off of Him. So, if I create what I want from what I say out of my mouth, and change the thoughts I have while increasing the power that lies in me God will release blessing in my life that is far above what I can ask or think.

Leave us with ONE word to describe a Mompreneur.

Inspiring!

A Woman's Worth Bio

Patricia Laurenceau is the Branding and Marketing Consultant of ReBrand to Profit (www.rebrandtoprofit.com) and your ReBrandologist where she helps womenpreneurs Unlock the Brand Within™ by gaining clarity, increasing visibility and expanding their reach. Patricia also is the host of Kickstart Your Brand Podcast (www.kickstartpodcast.com) where she provides strategies, tips and information on building a profitable brand, business and life you love.

Patricia started her mompreneur journey about 8 years ago after she had her daughter and had the opportunity to really work her business while on maternity leave. Several months before it was time for to return back to work and get a clear plan in place to leave her full-time job and run her business full time, she found out she was pregnant with her son.

Frustrated and overwhelmed because the process just got harder, Patricia decided to take the leap of faith and just JUMP! Now she can help other women entrepreneurs Unlock the Brand Within ™ them so they can live the life they were intended to live.

1. Empower, encourage and engage entrepreneurs and business owners.
2. Provide small business solutions that yield results.
3. Help women understand that a true entrepreneur pursues purpose, not money; knowing that when purpose is fulfilled, the money will come.
4. Create a community of entrepreneurs who are clear about their purpose so they can make a significant impact in the community around them.

Patricia feels her purpose is to make a significant difference in the world and to end brand failure one entrepreneur at a time. She is passionate about making sure that small businesses are successful and that they reach the audience that you were called to reach. She believes that your business **MUST** succeed because there is a large group of customers that are waiting for what you have to offer and she is committed to making that happen.

CHAPTER 10
LA JUAN HINES ROME

She' Matters Girls Inc. Founder/chief Executive Officer

Who is the Mompreneur behind the business? Tell us about you.

"Just like hope springing high, still I rise." Dr. Maya Angelou

DESPITE MY CIRCUMSTANCES, I REFUSE to look like what I've been through. I encourage you to remain determined! Be persistence and work to thrive always! Here is my story.

I am La Juan Hines-Rome, the oldest child of Ruby J. Strange and the 5th of nine grandchildren of the late Deacon and Deaconess James

Hines Sr. I never met or knew my biological father. I thought of myself as the "fatherless child". If it were not for my granddad and my oldest uncle, James "Poppa Hines" or "Uncle Brother," I would have been lost. I was born and raised in Norfolk, Virginia and later moved to Virginia Beach, Virginia with my Mom and brother in a house my Mom and step-dad had built. My life growing up in Virginia Beach was what some would consider privileged. A brand new two-story home, two new SUV Jeeps and an older model, well-equipped Volkswagen. In a two-parent home from appearances, we looked affluent. When my step-dad was out to sea, my mother, brother, aunts, cousins, and I enjoyed shopping most Saturdays after breakfast. My Mom kept a clean house, warm, open and inviting where friends enjoyed gathering every Friday night. Saturday family got together to eat, listen to music, play cards and just have a great time. My step-dad was in the NAVY on a submarine. When he was away, we lived well, laughed often and enjoyed life.

Our house was peaceful when he was away. When he returned, it was the sounds of old Motown R&B ballets that flooded the air. The records covered the living room floor where l, my brother and cousins would play board games while ease dropping on our parent's conversations. Instead of plates piled high with delicious foods, the kitchen table would have large white sheets of rolled graph paper of his blueprints, where he'd worked on building this or that. He always talked about and showed them to the sprinkle of family that would come by but it seemed he only talked about what he planned, never did we see him put his plans to action. His career title, I think was Engineer. He seemed to be knowledgeable about matters of Science, Math and upcoming technology that he'd studied. His career was also finding his way to my room in the early morning hours. When the house was quiet, I'd awake to him standing over my bed whispering my name with the nasty smell of cigarettes and coffee on his breath. Before I could say no, or leave me alone or get out of my room, I felt his callous hands on my legs then my thighs. When I moved too much for him, he'd squeeze my thighs so tight it felt like his fingers would penetrate my skin and rip apart my bones. When he climbed on my bed and did what he wanted to, he moved off and reminded me that if told, no one would believe me. Just as quietly as he entered, he left. Left me wide awake, crying, wondering why me, what did I do or say to make him believe he could do this to me, for years?

> *"Did you want to see me broken?*
> *Bowed head and lowered eyes? Shoulders falling down like teardrops,*
> *Weakened by my soulful cries?"* Dr. Maya Angelou

I refused to let my situations define me. His abuse began when I was young while we lived in Wellington Oaks in Norfolk, Virginia. When we moved to Virginia Beach, it continued. Many episodes of the abuse I cannot recall. As an adult, slight trigger such as a smell, the floor coloring or certain sounds forcefully bring the abuse back to mind. The last recollection of me locking my room door to prevent his entry was during a visit home from college. I remember not only locking my door but propping a chair under the door knob to prevent him from unlocking and still coming in.

Going to school in Virginia Beach was great; at school, I soared. While at Princess Anne Jr. High School, I proved every negative voice inside of me wrong by making the cheering squad, maintaining honors, and participating in various extracurricular clubs all so I would not have to go home. My time at school extended beyond the normal school day, especially when he was home. Once I found employment, my tension to find something to do to stay away from home further decreased.

To keep my mind off the dysfunction of my home life where my Mom's morning beverage changed from coffee to something much stronger, to our lights and or water being turned off every other month, to my brother and I having to fend for ourselves, I focused on "doing me!" My brother who is five years younger decided in his junior year of high school to drop-out of school to attend Job Corp. Me, I paid to take a summer school class to graduate a year early. My escape from that residence was my sole goal.

My plan worked. I kept busy with school work, activities, employment, volunteer experiences and hanging with friends. I graduated a year early from Green Run High School, with the class of 1989. Excited to begin my collegiate life at Virginia Commonwealth University (VCU) to major in  Mass Communication, I began to pack. Moving into Johnson Hall on campus was like a whole new world. Oh, how I loved going to school there and the freedom and independence it offered was refreshing. Living in Richmond, I too enjoyed. I did not have to report to anyone nor was I worried about waking to find someone standing over my bed in the middle of the night. I believed the heavens were shining on me and that great things were truly working out in my favor. As usual, my grades were most important, but what I also found was that I enjoyed being with the opposite sex. I became promiscuous. During high school, I was a tease. I enjoyed the attention of the guys and loved to flirt. I believe I lost my virginity at age 18. While in school at VCU, I had a male friend there, one in North Carolina and another back home. The betrayal of my body I'd experienced as a child during the abuse, I no longer felt when with the guys of my choice. Whether it was through close body proximity or sexual intercourse, I thoroughly enjoyed the feeling of power and control I commanded. I felt in power thinking what I gave or did not give made a difference for them. Their attention validated me. I did not feel alone until my calls to them went unanswered. Hence,

I doubted myself more. I felt less of a person because of what I was doing. Little did I know my demonstration of such behaviors was due to not fully knowing my worth.

When my financial assistance no longer covered housing, I transferred home to finish my Bachelor of Science degree from Old Dominion University (ODU) in Speech Communication. During one of my return visits home, I broke the silence and told my Mom what was going on. We talked but I've never felt true closure. In 1992 after moving back to Norfolk, my Uncle made it possible for me to move into one of his rentals. In 1993, I achieved what I thought was not possible, I was accepted into the illustrious Delta Sigma Theta Sorority, Inc. In 1994, I received my Bachelor of Science (BS) degree and months later meet my best friend, the man I would soon wed. Before deciding to receive my Master's degree, I decided to send letters to *Harpo Productions* and the television series of *You Bet Your Life,* a remake of the 1950-1961 game show hosted by Bill Cosby. When there was no immediate response, I continued to pursue my writing dream. While sitting in a hair salon, I picked up *InSyte Magazine.* The cover displayed a large black and white photo of Malcolm X for the month of February. I reviewed and enjoyed the articles and thought, I could do this. So, I contacted the Editor in Chief, Alonzo Brandon. In our discussion, he asked me of my expected pay. I'd never been paid to write, so I was unsure of what to say. Yes, I'd researched pay prior to, but I had no idea he'd ask me this in our first phone call. When he quoted me my rate per word and then explained my story I was pleased and excited yet nervous. In May of 1994, I'd graduated college with my BS degree, arranged to interview a loan officer for Harbor Mortgage in downtown Norfolk for one of my largest stories and met my best friend; the man I've spent the last 23 years of my life with, (Dr.) Garry A. Rome. That two-year writing opportunity opened doors of continued possibilities for me. I met a lot of significant people and learned greatly about myself and my craft. Interviewing members of the community for story leads increased my level of esteem. Having my writing accepted and being published month after month increased my confidence. Here I was doing what someone early on told me I would never do, write. Not only was I writing, but I was being paid to do what I loved. That experience led me to *The Virginian Pilot's Compass* where I freelanced for Michael Knepler. Did I ever hear from Harpo Productions or You Bet Your Life? Yes, I did. Their confirmations although acknowledged no vacancies, were reassuring. It provided me a greater sense of confidence to continue pursuing my writing and the credit that proved I could achieve.

Life got real! In 1996 I married my best friend Garry in Norfolk, VA and two years later our son Khalil was born. Motherhood, what a wonderful joy. Two years later we discovered we'd have another bundle of joy joining our family. WOW! Look at me. I couldn't believe my body was able to create such beautiful beings. Nor did I believe that I had enough love to give to our new baby girl because I felt our son had all my love. Not recognizing just how God expands that flap of love to make room for more, when my baby girl, Jordan was born, I felt the expansion. I was now the mother of two beautiful babies. I felt so empowered and complete. I had achieved something many women only dream of, childbirth. I was grateful and together the four of us were happy!

Five years later, we experienced a major financial storm. My husband lost his job; as a result, our income was reduced significantly causing us to lose our townhome. This tragedy caused us to move into his parent's home. This of course was not where I wanted to be, but I was thankful to have shelter. During the four years there I learned more about me and recognized who I needed to be for my children. Motherhood is an amazing, fulfilling and an enriched experience. If God is not your center, evil can penetrate your mind and influence your thoughts. My marriage was strained. We argued and rarely spoke unless it dealt with the children. I wanted to throw in the towel but death changed us. His father had passed before we moved in from pancreatic cancer. Years later, while living with his Mom, my grandmother was diagnosed with dementia and passed. Seven months after her passing, my Uncle who'd cared for me like I was his own passed away. Less than eight months after him, my grandfather passed. My world was flipped upside down. But all was not lost. In the midst of it all, I discovered I was pregnant with our third child and our search for a rental turned into the closing of our first home. Elated about the blessing, we were now homeowners. Again, I believe heaven was smiling on me. Of course, now, there were three angles aside of God to guide and whisper to my heart what they'd always done to encourage and support me.

In 2004, while teaching at Lake Taylor High School, my husband and I agreed to assist one of my students. We were not able to financially assist Terrell, but we provided him all the love and support parents would provide their child. Bringing him into our family was an easy task. Terrell was open minded, ready and hungry for support. With God's grace and mercy, with the assistance if his second adoptive dad, helped him through Virginia State University (VSU). He's now 30 years old and works as a Correction Sergeant in Jarrett, VA. In 2007, I began working at Booker T. Washington High School in Norfolk, VA as the Transition Advisor. In 2008, our third bundle arrived, a beautiful baby girl, Logan. Our circle was complete. Until a few years later, 2009, my husband and I agreed to assist another one of my students. Shamyra was a junior high school student whose family dynamics were unique. She lived with us through her senior year of high school and the four years of college at VSU (her choice). Our immediate family of five quickly turned to seven. Shamyra taught us a lot and prepared my husband and me for future experiences with our own. She is now a Deputy Sheriff in Richmond, VA

"Out of the huts of history's shame ...
Up from a past that's rooted in pain, I rise.
Leaving behind nights of terror and fear ...
Into a daybreak that's wondrously clear, I rise.
Dr. Maya Angelou

As the mother of four at home; my son was in middle school, so my focus was on our three girls. My husband had my son active in sports. With a high school senior, a rising sixth grader and a preschooler, my hands were full. I recognized my rising middle schooler was dealing with bullying while my high schooler dealt with misunderstanding her worth. The bullying issues and my oldest dating guys that did not treat her like a queen greatly alarmed me. Conversations with other parents rendered the same or similar distress with their daughters. What could have been taken care of with our daughters in a normal sleep over or skate party turned into creating an organization for girls dealing with similar issues. As a result, in 2011, I developed She' Matters G.I.R.L.S. (SMG), LLC an organization to provide pre-teens a vehicle to learn about themselves, value their image, and increase their esteem but most importantly, to teach them their worth. Research states that over 70% of girls' age 15 to 17 avoid normal daily activities, such as attending school, when they feel bad about their looks. With 75% of girls having low self-esteem, research state girls engage in negative activities like cutting, bullying, smoking, drinking, or disordered eating when they feel they do not fit in. This compares to 25% of girls with high self-esteem. This is not what I wanted for my daughters or anyone else's so I set up to develop workshops and forums that brought in professional educators, social workers and other business owners who could give our daughters what they needed to understand who they are.

"SMG" was developed because I knew although my daughters listened when we had our "real talk" times, I observed how well and more intrigued they were to receive the same information from my best girlfriends like Annette. Annette and I were childhood friends. We were cheer sisters since seventh grade. When we talk with our girls, we share the same information but they received it differently coming from her. Seeing this, I believed the format to bring in others would work best. Today, Annette is the organization's Deputy Director and her 14-year-old daughter, Danielle with my 17-year-old daughter Jordan and 9-year-old Logan are all a part of our Junior Executive Team.

The time from 2011 to 2013 were challenging for us at SMG. Although our workshops and trainings were well received and attended we wanted to provide so much more. Our programs were being funded from donations from friends and family and of course, ourselves. Even though we were LLC, we were not successful with receiving grants. It was then that I believed being incorporated would assist us greater. Just as our acronym says, we are *Girls Who Inspire and Refine Limitless Standards,* I set out to do what I would have thought was a joke years earlier. I completed our 501c3 information with my communication degree and no business knowledge. I asked a lot of questions and leaned on the knowledge and background of my husband to make this happen.

In February, She' Matters GIRLS, Inc. will celebrate our sixth anniversary. The journey was no easy task. My husband and I lost our home in 2011, we came close to separating, rather divorcing and in the process, we uprooted our family more than twice to live with relatives until we found a place where we could all be together. During this time, my husband realized he needed to make a change in his life for his health first and then for us. Nearly dropping 100 lbs. has changed him as a man of God and a husband. He's also a greater dad. He and I are in a two-year leadership course at our church which is bringing us closer together and closer to Christ. The weight lost not only helped our marriage tremendously, but piecing together our marriage has brought triumph to our entire family.

Being a Mompreneur does not mean that you have all the answers. Yes, we do wear the "S" on our chest but we must remember that we do not have to be all things to all people. Being a successful Mompreneur means you know how to seek assistance when needed. After two years of applying for grants and being turned down, we are now awaiting confirmation for our first grantor via bank funding.

What made you decide to start the business that you're in?
My middle daughter was entering middle school. The summer before starting 6th grade and one of her friends had a sleepover. They attended a K-8 school so many of them were friends since kindergarten. I had noticed a difference in my daughter's interactions with a few of the girls so I asked her about it. She shared how she'd been teased about her weight or how they treated her indifferent. When we met with the girls and their parents for the sleepover, I shared my concerns with the mothers. Together we called in the girls involved and discussed our concerns of bullying. The girls apologized, made up and returned as friends. Although this situation was taken care of, other issues in different shadows followed. At the same time, our oldest daughter, Shamyra was dealing with relationship issues with the young man she was dating. I saw how he spoke to her, how he held working on her car as collateral for her continuing to see him. They would argue then break up and be back together days later. Enough was enough. My girls needed more teaching on how to recognize their self-esteem and confidence in helping them understand their worth. Their situations were reasons She' Matters GIRLS was created.

What made you LEAP? How did you make the leap from a secure paid job to starting your own business?

My leap was due to the need of my girls. They listened to me but received the message better from others, especially when they realized they were not the only ones dealing with such issues. Their well-being and emotional self was essential to me. Despite their past, I wanted them to be well balanced, confident girls and young women. I wanted them to be individuals who recognized their voices and realized that they could speak up for themselves without guilt or shame.

How do you balance or how did you balance your work/home life?

Through God's grace and mercy and the help of my husband I have been able to balance my work career as an educator, our family life and my organization. I knew very little about "business" or how to run a business. I knew how to run a household and had 12 years of doing that with success. I visualized early what I wanted in my business and my husband helped me develop it from obtaining my LLC to later gaining 501c3. He's assisted me with fundraising, board dynamics and program ideas. In the beginning years of development, my family had begun to ask if "they mattered" because I spent so much time with She' Matters GIRLS. Even my husband would ask if there was a "HE Matters". However, once he realized that together we could do this and make it work, our home life with everyone going in their own directions went smoother. Having a cohesive executive team is exceptionally important as well. The outcome must be the same for everyone involved.

What do you say to yourself when you feel like giving up? What keeps you going?

Our daughters need this service. Whenever I feel a hiatus is necessary, God places someone else in my path through an email, a phone call or an inbox message to share about the struggles their daughters are going through. He allows me to see that what we have is valuable and through our service, others are learning to recognize their worth.

What was the best advice you ever received? Worst advice?

We have yet to receive directly any bad advice. Our best advice has always been in the form of thank you. Thank you for making a difference in "her" life. Our mantra is we are –

Committed to grooming natural leaders!
Dedicated to making a difference in the lives of our daughters!

We All know the saying It takes a village to raise a child, but for a mom starting her own business, the village may be a state. So who do you turn to or go to for help? Who are your go-to people/services?

For help, I go to those I know who have had previous experience with what I'm dealing with. Especially if I know they've had success in doing it, I seek advice and support from them. For further support, depending on the topic, I go to family and close friends. They are truly my rock!

What do you do to unwind and recharge? How important is this for a Mompreneur?

Music soothes me. Regardless of what I'm dealing with, I crank up the music. Yolanda Adams, Anita Wilson, Kierra Clark Sheard or Kem, Algebra Blassett, Lelah and Donny Hathaway and so many others either calm or recharge me to continue the fight. This and prayer is my refuge. Through it all, I make sure to give Christ the praise. All I do, I do for His glory. How important is this for a mompreneur? Taking care of self, mentally, spiritually, emotionally and physically is essential. Balance in my life is necessary for me to not only accomplish my goal but to ensure that it's maintained. Truly, this is a challenging task, juggling being a wife, mother, daughter and career professional and an entrepreneur, but I make myself take time for me when I need it even if it's a few hours a day.

What book would you recommend for a Mompreneur just starting out? Why this particular one?

Scriptures and stories from the Bible have become my main source of reference for guidance. Besides the Bible, I would recommend anything that's inspirational and that speaks to your heart.

What are some of the ways that you involve or have involved your family in your business?

My immediate family, husband, and children are involved with the organization from A – Z. My daughters head the Jr. Executive Team of girls. Their participation is crucial to ensure we are focusing on what their peers need at their levels. We want to hit not miss the mark. My son assists with marketing and promotion and, when available, he and my husband assist with set up and break down of our events. My husband also cooks for our family. So, on several occasions, we've solicited him to make his gourmet specials. Everyone in the family has worked the business at some time.

What did it feel like to make your first dollar as a Mompreneur? How long did that take?

Our first dollar was made during our premier workshop, but that was not our greatest "ah-ha". Our greatest moment happened in 2014, two years after receiving our incorporation when the President of Freedom Ford dealership blessed us with a $1,000 donation. For us, this was gold. Since starting, we had not received a donation of that amount. His contribution spoke volumes to validate our work. Although he is no longer with that dealership, he's still a financial supporter and for that and more, we are grateful!

Kids & Significant others, do and say the darndest things. Please share with us one of your funniest moments, embarrassing moments, saddest moments, and most rewarding moment that involving your family and your business?

The most frustrating, perhaps saddest moment for me was to have my daughter experience a tragedy. Her behavior surprised both my husband and I and my business partner. What she did was totally against what we teach. Knowing she believes in who she is and whose she is had always assured us she knew better. However, the enemy is busy. Do understand if he cannot get to you, he will work to be successful in your children. Initially, I thought how I am going to inspire and encourage others when I can't seem to do it for my own when she needs me most. Her cry had nothing to do with me or my status, but everything to do with what God wanted from me, from us. She felt stressed and lacked our support. Although, I strive to not raise mine the way in which I was raised, at times, old parenting techniques rear its head, causing me to yell and not quiet myself to listen and reach a solution. I am working on me! By God's grace and mercy, our daughter is doing better.

What is Your Favorite Quote?

It's better to give than to receive. We teach the principle of how having a closed fist vs an open hand blocks your blessings. Keeping your hand closed nothing goes out, but nothing can come in. Keeping it open, blessings can flow openly. We help our daughters understand that we give not to receive but because it's the right thing to do!

Leave us with ONE word to describe a Mompreneur.

DETERMINED

To be determined is to be unwavering, strong minded, firm, controlled. To be successful, you must do something you've never done, step out on faith. Being determined keeps you focused and on course. It's your time! I believe in you! You're worth it! Now go get it!

CHAPTER 11

NIKKIA SMITH

Founder & Ceo At Hearts Full Of Grace

Who is the Mompreneur behind the business? Tell us about you.

IT TOOK ME MANY YEARS to finally realize who I truly am! The moment that I sat up in my bed, having figured it all out, was one of the happiest days of my life. I accepted that I was exactly who God had called me to be and that reality made all the difference in the world to myself, to my children, to my relationships and to my business.

I am a mother and a pretty awesome one at that. I have four beautiful, brilliant, outstanding children. I have made mistakes as a parent but fortunately, I have learned from each of them. My children are the greatest joy God has afforded me and I do not take the job I have as their mother lightly. Alexis is my oldest child and my only daughter. She is currently in Law School and I often say that God placed her in my life to save me. I was a freshman in college when she was born. I doubted my ability to be the mother she deserved, but I remember having a conversation with my sister friend Rochelle and my Aunt Gladys. Rochelle encouraged me to raise a "World Changer" and indeed Alexis is. My aunt simply promised me that everything would be alright. As I gave birth to Alexis, my Aunt Gladys held one leg while my mother held the other. Off to the left of me, Alexis's Nana whispered these words to me: "Nik, she's going to be very forceful." As my mother took her first grandchild into her arms, I watched her stare at her soft skin and her bright eyes. From that day on, Alexis would be her pride and joy. Thank God they each saw something in me that at the time, I didn't see in myself. Thank God they took the time to speak into a life that I wasn't sure I was equipped to raise. As Alexis grew however, I began to realize that God had equipped me to be her mother from the very beginning.

Twelve years later, I had Xavier. I had been working for years as a Teacher, his father and I were in love and I felt prepared to be his mother. Xavier was a happy baby, his smile lit up the room. He was my little King. Four years later tragedy would strike our lives and I would learn that while he looked very much like me he was clothed in strength just like his father. Xavier is this humble guy who takes care of his family, respects others, and knows everything there is to know about animals. He dreams of being a paleontologist.

Two years after Xavier entered the world, my womb was stretched to the max and I pushed out my twin boys, Joshua and Tarran. The twins are best friends! I watch them and learn so much about loyalty and commitment. They plan to become engineers and own a restaurant. I remember the years I spent at home with the boys. I felt like all I did was breastfeed, change soiled pampers, read books and listen to The Wiggles. Well, the reality was that I did all those things and so much more! I was a mother and at the time, a wife so my job was huge! I had the most rewarding job imaginable. The smiles, the laughter, the growth made my job so much easier. It took an entire year before the twins were on the same schedule and while I struggled to get them there, I spent many nights crying in the bed. No one heard my cries, I kept them silent and hidden because I didn't want to bother anyone, not even their father who was working multiple jobs at the time to take care of our family. I suffered in silence, but the day they finally got on a schedule, marked a day of rejoicing! My children are the reason I committed my life to fighting, even against the worst of all odds. They are the center of my life. Their presence allowed me to realize my purpose. My life has been built around preparing them to become awesome citizens who are responsible, compassionate, and lovers of God.

AM healed. I spent so many years broken and hurt. One day, God introduced me to my destiny and I learned that in order to fully walk into it, I had to undergo a process of healing. It took years, but it was worth the time I devoted to undergoing the process.

I AM free. There were days when I felt as if I were in prison. My mind was so troubled that I was a captive in my own body. Thank God, I chose to unlock my prison door and bask in the freedom that naturally belonged to me.

I AM not defined by my past. Once I accepted that my past was not reflective of my future, it made everything about my life better. I used to look back over my life and be ashamed. I would cry over the poor decisions I'd made. I had faulted myself for the abuse I had undergone at the hands of my babysitter's son. I was bitter and broken. As some would say, I was a hot mess! To God Be the Glory, I am not who I used to be. When I look at myself in the mirror, I am happy with who I am today! Even if I look in the mirror and see a pimple on my face, it doesn't matter to me! I would rather see 100 pimples than to see the pieces of a broken me that I used to see!

I AM a Mama's Girl. My mom gave birth to me and said that's it! I understand why. I imagine she knew that I was going to make her life difficult at times and indeed I did. She never gave up on me though, not ever. I know I broke her heart, I know there were times when I disappointed her, but she never let me know it. She was and continues to be right there for me whenever I call. I know a number of women who struggled to have a healthy relationship with their mothers. While, there were bumps in the road along the way, what she established with me, helped me to establish something amazing with my own daughter. I am simply blessed to have my mother!

I AM a woman of Great faith. I have made decisions based wholly on the fact that I believe in God. I have never regretted any decision I have made based on the activation of my faith. God never fails me! I have to repeat that, God NEVER fails me!

I AM a business owner. I remember chuckling the first time I was introduced as a CEO and founder. They are really talking about me I thought.

I AM an engaged woman! No, he doesn't define me and is not yet my husband, but the relationship God has allowed us to develop has certainly made me a better woman. I have to admit, I didn't make it extremely easy for him, but he didn't give up on me. When I pray at night, I thank God for saving him just for me!

I AM an Intercessor. God has called me to pray for others and that's just what I do. I spend a tremendous portion of my day in prayer for others. We all have special gifts and talents and while the life of a mother, business owner, fiancé and prayer warrior can get challenging, it is all worth it!

I AM a conqueror! God put the right people in my life as a child to pour strength and wisdom into my spirit. I watched my grandmother, my mother, and my aunts personify strength. It's in my blood. Even greater than being raised by phenomenal women who taught me how to overcome, God called said so!!

Every morning, I affirm myself before I venture to start my day. It's important to me to begin each day in prayer, meditation, and affirmation. These habits have proven to be extremely effective in helping me to live out the person I am destined to be.

What made you decide to start the business that you're in?

It was October 2009, the day before my daughter turned 16. Her aunts had planned a grand Sweet 16 Celebration and we were both excited! We had spent the entire day at Alexis's Debate Competition. Once we arrived home that evening, we were exhausted! After I spent some time with my boys, I showered and was so happy to climb into the bed. Hours later, I received a phone  call that the man I had vowed to spend my life with I had never even considered a life without him had been shot. I arrived at the hospital pleading with the staff to see him only to be told that "it [was] too late to see him." He had not survived the gunshot wounds. The man who I had vowed to spend my life with had been murdered. I had to go home and tell my children that their father would not be coming home.

I spent the two months that followed the murder swallowed up in a period of indescribable pain. My heart had been broken and I sunk into depression. I cried, I lost weight, I didn't cook, my best friend had to stay at my house to ensure that my sons were bathed and fed. At that time, I honestly thought that I wasn't going to make it through this ordeal. One day however, I did the only thing that I could do; I prayed! I believe that God had been waiting to hear from me because my life changed completely that day. I prayed that God would heal me. I cried out to him: "I need you; I can't do this on my own!" I felt God saying that my healing would come through helping others. Naturally, I was baffled. I thought to myself, "Don't I already help people?" I had received the revelation from God but didn't quite understand. I returned to work that day as a Preschool Teacher. As I entered my classroom to look over the upcoming theme, I almost started screaming! The following week, I was to focus on Caring and Sharing as a theme. "Wow God!" I thought. "You work fast!"

To help make the connection of caring and sharing with my students, I organized a canned food drive. It was largely successful. In class, we discussed ways to help people, the benefits of helping others. The Food Drive was an ultimate expression of helping and caring for others. The word spread throughout the other preschool programs and soon we were preparing baskets for families at other schools. I saw the faces of the families receiving the baskets and I knew that I had to do more. After the drive officially ended, I began preparing sandwiches, snack bags, and toiletry bags for adults who struggled with hunger and homelessness themselves. I began serving others at least once a month. Eventually, I had to find a name for my organization. That was it! My business had been birthed!

In time, it would grow to help adults in children in various capacities. I often joke and call it my 5th child. Just like each of my deliveries, the process was painful but well worth it!

What made you LEAP? How did you make the leap from a secure paid job to starting your own business?
I'm sure you have noticed that I am a woman who takes my spirituality seriously. With that awareness, it should be easy to understand that much of my decision to LEAP from a secure job came as a result of a number of spiritual indicators.

I had spent 18 years in the classroom. I spent time teach middle school, high school, preschool, alternative school, English and History throughout the course of my exciting career as an educator. There was never a question that God designed me to teach. I was outstanding in my field. My students loved and trusted me and I loved sharing my craft with them. I was creative, energetic, relatable and I made learning fun and engaging. As a single parent with three young sons, however; teaching had become overwhelming. I would spend all day being the mother, teacher, nurse, and caregiver to a room full of beautiful children who I without a doubt loved and treated them as if they were my own children. I gave them everything that I had to give each day that I was in the classroom. Unfortunately, I arrived home feeling depleted and burnt out! I found myself feeling as if my children were paying an unfair price because of my dedication. In November 2015, while heading to a meeting, I took a moment and prayed. I told God that I felt as if I were cheating my children out of valuable time with me. In my prayer, I asked HIM to let me know if I could be released from that position. I ended my prayer with an Amen and walked into my meeting. During the meeting, the Executive Director of the program delivered an announcement. Our program was ending the following June. He advised us during his message, to seek other jobs! The room was filled with Preschool Teachers, Assistants, and Counselors who had no idea what they were going to do. I, on the other hand couldn't hide my delight! I was being released!

I had children so I knew that I needed to work, or at least I thought that I did. I went to a job fair and landed a job almost immediately after the announcement that the preschool program was ending. This new job, I felt would allow me to work, care for my children financially, and not drain me to the point that I would feel useless once I got home. It didn't take long before new pressures started to emerge. I started meeting some of the most remarkable Christian women around but I was miserable. I remember going home one evening and telling my daughter that I just wanted to do Hearts Full of Grace full time. My daughter has always been my greatest supporter and advocate so naturally her advice to me was simply, "well you should do that then mom."

The following day at work, one of my colleagues told me that she saw mw in a dream. She explained the dream and then offered her interpretation of the dream to me. She said, "You are called to serve and that is what God wants you to do. Anything outside of your organization is a distraction." I heard those words playing over and over again in my head for the remainder of the day. The next day, one of my best friends came to the job to drop off a donation for Hearts Full of Grace. We stood in the parking lot for a while and before she left, she handed me a CD. It was a message from a recent women's conference at her church. She looked at me and said: "I believe that God wants you to hear this." I returned to my desk and inserted the CD. I placed my headphones on and quickly began to enjoy the message. Then the tempo in the presenter's voice changes, as if she has something more important than anything that she has already said. I said up in my chair, adjusted my headphones to be sure that I didn't miss this profound statement. When she uttered the words, I almost fell out of my seat! The speaker on the cd advised her listeners to "let go of the distractions!" She continued by advising that we rid ourselves of anything that served as a distraction from doing what God had called us to do in our lives. I played it over and over again, just to be certain that I had heard her correctly. Well, I had heard her correctly, but I wasn't ready to accept that that message was for me.

Finally, the evening was almost over and I took a call from a student. He was calling from Texas. His voice was deep and authoritative. He was a minister. We had never spoken before and he knew nothing about me, yet he would be the next person to speak into my future. "Nikkia, my spirit is telling me that you are not where you are supposed to be. Your job is a distraction. I hope you will take some time and pray." At that point, I didn't need to hear it again. I was in the wrong place. I wasn't going to waste any more time with distractions. God called me to serve and I had accepted that calling in 2009. Now, six years later, I was preparing myself to take a huge leap of faith. A very good friend of mine called me in December, prior to my leaving the classroom. She recommended that I begin to save my money. That advice was based on a dream she had had about me. In our conversation she said, "God told me to tell you to save your money. I don't know why but I am being obedient." I headed her advice and saved my money. On May 2016, I left my job and began working full time for Hearts Full of Grace!

How do you balance or how did you balance your work/home life?
Balance, what's that? □ the dictionary defines balance as an EQUAL distribution of weight. A condition in which different elements are equal, or in the correct proportions.

If my answer is based on #1, I would say that I don't actually balance at all. I can never distribute the "weight" of my life equally because my children will always deserve more of me than anything else. While I consider my business as my 5th child, that is merely a figure of speech. I devote a tremendous amount of time to my business but I have always devoted more to my children and my relationship with God.

If my answer were to be based on definition #2, I would say YES, there is such a thing as balance. The elements in my life are proportioned, based on their relevance in my life. Hearts Full of Grace is a priority just as my children are, just as my relationship with God is.

Now, the reality of my life is this: sometimes I balance well and sometimes I completely do a horrible job. With years of practice I must say that the good times far outweigh the tough times. Everything has a place and as of this year, everything has a day. There are certain days when I refuse to conduct business unless it is an absolute emergency. On those days, I am sure to maximize time with my children and my future hubby (yes I am in love)! On those days, when no business is allowed, we have as much fun together as possible. With my sons, it may be a movie or bowling. With my daughter, it may be shopping or a museum. With my sweetie, it may be live music and crab cakes. My family is always first. Additionally, nothing interferes with my prayer and alone time with God. I tend to spend those moments when my children are asleep, either early in the morning or late at night. I love spontaneous interactions so when I mention that everything has a day, that doesn't mean that I may decide to work on an "off" day. I just ensure that my children do not miss out when I make adjustments.

Having a family and running a business can be a challenge. Ultimately, balance is achieved when you organize your life and structure it in a manner where you can be consistent and your children and/ or mate, and your spirituality are always a priority and never sacrificed completely.

What do you say to yourself when you feel like giving up? What keeps you going?

I believe that we all have those moments when there appears to be so much going on in our lives that it would be easier to let it all go and give up! Fortunately, I was raised by a group of strong women who never gave up, no matter the odds. The foundation that my grandmother, mother, and aunts established for me always comes to mind when I feel like it would be easier to just walk away. More importantly, I think about my children. What message would I send to them if they saw me giving up? They are taught that giving up is not a choice. You may have to start over, you may have to redesign the plan, but you never give up, in one way or the other, you finish it!

I think about my favorite bible verse, "I can do ALL things through Christ who gives me strength" when I am on the brink of letting it go. I think about my children and the fact that every single step I take, they see and they follow. My life is my message to them. The way I handle situations is the model they follow. I am preparing a legacy for them and they will not see me quit,

What was the best advice you ever received? Worst advice?

Trust God

Once I reached a place in my life where I decided to align everything I did with God's will for my destiny, everything started falling into place. I began the process of healing. Unhealthy friendships and relationships ended. Doors began to open that I had only dreamed of walking through. Bills were paid, even without a job that paid a salary. I found myself functioning in overflow mode, not only was there enough to sustain me and my family, but there was more than enough.

We All know the saying It takes a village to raise a child, but for a mom starting her own business, the village may be a state. So who do you turn to or go to for help? Who are your go-to people/services?
We all need someone to turn to for help. I am blessed that I don't have to turn very far. My children are exceptional. The bulk of the work that is done in my business is charitable. Whenever there is a scheduled outreach, I don't even have to ask, my children are waiting to support me. They know me so well that they can feel my energy. My children are always the first to step in, especially my oldest two, Alexis and Xavier. They support me with patience and they just do whatever needs to be done. They each have very busy and demanding schedules themselves but they love me and believe in me, so they willingly support the mission of Hearts Full of Grace. Whenever there is an outreach planned or I have to facilitate a workshop or training, I can always rest assured that my babies have my back! Yes, they are my babies and even though my oldest daughter is nearly 24, she is my baby as well.

My daughter helps me with anything that requires a technological touch and my son Xavier ensures that I don't have to engage in too much manual labor. He is such a gentleman. The twins fill in wherever needed. Often they support Xavier with packing, sorting, and transporting items. Before we conduct a feeding, we load 3 trucks and a car. My daughter has always been my rock in this endeavor. When everyone else doubted me, she was the one person who always believed in me! Alexis is truly my greatest advocate. There is so much work that goes into preparing for our outreaches, so much time and effort that goes into supporting my dream, I know that God was demonstrating HIS love for me when he chose to give me the four children that I have.

My mother is always there as well. She may pick up or drop off donations, help to organize the storage, facilitate our feeding outreach, reach out for sponsorship, run off copies for a workshop, she is just my Superwoman! Sometimes she may support me by simply taking the boys to a movie when I have a speaking engagement or have an empowerment workshop to facilitate. Whatever the task, she is there and she is willing. I thank God for my mom, she truly is the best.

My fiancé is someone else I call on rather frequently. At a recent Appreciation Luncheon for my volunteers, I jokingly said that he had no idea what he was getting into when we started dating. Truly, the dynamics of my life were different from many but he has been my Knight in Shining Armor. He assures me that I never have to do it alone. The nature of my business requires lifting, traveling, setting up, etc. He calls himself "the heavy box lifter." I often laugh when he says it, but deep down inside, I am grateful that God deemed us (me and my children) worthy of a man who helps whenever and wherever he can, in an effort to lighten my load.

I am fortunate to be aligned with some amazing women; I refer to them as Team Hearts Full of Grace. They know that I will work hard all alone before I call them, but in the end, I often end up calling them and they always come through. I love these ladies: Cynthia, Sonja, Paula, Chavon, Waltika, Shontail, Shelita and Quita! Collectively, we wear many hats as a Non-Profit Organization but the ladies who work with me are my sisters, of course we aren't related by blood but I have always believed that family is weakly defined if only defined by blood relation.

There are also two women who support the organization and I spiritually and financially. They are two of the most successful and intelligent women I know, Danita and Katrina. Danita is my organizations major sponsor and a phenomenal businesswoman. The story of our friendship is so cool. In Junior High School, we were rappers and built an unbreakable bond at that time. Katrina is also a longtime friend as well who has this unmatched ability to pour into me and pray for me. I have dubbed her my "Spiritual Coach." Many times, I receive a call from her at precisely the right time! It is amazing to be connected to such extraordinary people!

Finally, my boy's grandparents are amazing! There are times when Papa Duke just shows up and loves on my boys. I can call on Mama Pam as I affectionately call her and pour my heart out to her and she freely listens and advises me. Sometimes when I am speaking with her, I am amazed at her strength and it makes sense why her son was as strong as he was…and why my sons are as strong as they are!

What do you do to unwind and recharge? How important is this for a Mompreneur?
This may be one of the most important things to ensure that we do as mompreneurs. We give so much of ourselves to our families, our churches, our communities, and our businesses. If we don't unwind and recharge, we could find ourselves worn out. Self-preservation is vital. I learned the hard way. I was working so hard, trying to "balance" it all, giving myself to everyone, pouring out and not taking the time to be poured into. I was so focused on doing it all because I felt that I could. The truth is I can do it all but not all in the same day or at the same time. At some point, I have to stop, breathe and relax. So, now, I make a conscious effort to do just that. A super-hot shower, a refreshing class of strawberry lemonade with ice and one of my many devotional books in hand is one of the ways I like to unwind. On a very good day, I love a massage and a pedicure. On an exceptional day, I love to sit near the beach and listen to the waves beat upon the sand. The sound is so tranquil and it allows me the freedom to just think about things. The best night ever, is relaxing on my couch with my children and fiancé, watching a movie.

What book would you recommend for a Mompreneur just starting out? Why this particular one?

I would recommend that a Mompreneur just starting out read any of the following books for much needed guidance and growth.

    a.   In the Company of Women by Grace Bonney
    b.   The 15 Invaluable Laws of Growth by John Maxwell
    c.   Destiny: Stepping into Your Purpose by T.D. Jakes

What are some of the ways that you involve or have involved your family in your business?

My family is extremely involved in my business. My children, my mother, and my fiancé work extremely hard to ensure that they are with me all the way. All of what Hearts Full of Grace does involves giving back to the community. There are seven programs functioning at the same time. Sometimes there is an outreach scheduled such as providing a meal for homeless youth and an empowerment workshop for women completing a reentry program in the same day. My daughter will generally help ensure that the printed materials, Power Points and interactive components are in place. My mother generally guarantees that the items needed for set up and distribution are in the proper containers and ready to be loaded. My fiancé and Xavier lift and load primarily, but they lend their hands anywhere they are needed. My twins, Joshua and Tarran help prepare toiletry and snack bags that will be distributed. On outreach days, my entire family joins me and assists in the outreach.

My family means everything to me! A strong support system is essential to our elevation as Mompreneurs. We cannot do it alone and even if we could, why should we want to?

What did it feel like to make your first dollar as a Mompreneur? How long did that take?

The nature of my business put me in contact with money fairly immediately. I have always put everything back into the nonprofit however.

The first time I received a $100 donation I nearly screamed! I was so excited. It wasn't mine, but it was for my vision and that made me so happy. When I finally decided to incorporate Hearts Full of Grace, my Board of Directors stipulated a percentage of cash donations be for my salary. Well, that's the only way I was going to make money from my business right? Not actually. I never allowed myself to receive a salary and I stand on my decision to do that. What I decided to do was incorporate some fee-based services that Hearts Full of Grace provides. I had been providing these services such as consulting, nonprofit event planning, tutoring, and workshops for free. Essentially, I was working for peanuts! Thanks to the guidance of two very wise women, I stopped cheating my children and I and began getting paid for some of the services Hearts Full of Grace provides. It had taken me six years to decide to do this. The first time I actually made money, I felt like I was floating on a cloud. I said, "Wow! I just got paid to do what I love to do!" I had been asked to speak at a Women's Empowerment event. My entire presentation was about an hour and I was paid $80. I tried to remain calm, I knew $80 wasn't much, but it was the first time I had been paid as an Executive Director and I was rejoicing because I knew that that $80 was just the beginning!

Kids & Significant others, do and say the darndest things. Please share with us one of your funniest moments, embarrassing moments, saddest moments, and most rewarding moment that involving your family and your business?

Much of our work is done in service to people experiencing homelessness. One afternoon we were out providing socks and blankets to some of our friends without homes. I was talking to a couple who'd lost their home. I asked them if they had followed up with a woman who could provide them with housing. The gentleman said, "I won't be able to use my phone until the end of the month." My twins heard the interaction and Tarran looked up at me and said, "Mom, can't they use your phone?" Joshua followed with: "Can they just live with us?" At that very moment I was so proud of the compassion my children had exhibited towards those we serve. The entire ride home they inundated me with questions about hunger and homelessness. They expressed their desire to help people in need wherever we may go. I allowed the gentleman to use my phone and they were connected with resources and were able to move into their own home!

What is Your Favorite Quote?
"Everybody can be great because anybody can serve...You only need a HEART FULL OF GRACE. A soul generated by love." Dr. Martin Luther King, Jr

This is the quote that inspired the name of my 5th child, my business, and my nonprofit. God called me for service because he knew that my soul was generated by love and that my heart was full of grace.

Leave us with ONE word to describe a Mompreneur.
Resolute! Mompreneurs are admirably purposeful, determined and unwavering!

CHAPTER 12

MARQUETA PLUM JENKINS

President & CEO At Makeda Builders LLC

Who is the Mompreneur behind the business? Tell us about you.

I USED TO ALWAYS ASK the question, "Why Me, Lord?" When I finally go to a place where I could hear Him speak back, He answered quietly and gently, "Why not you?" We often wonder why we go through what we do in life, but as a believer we have an obligation to "deny ourselves" and take up our crosses designed for us to bear. I learned early on that we deal with life's challenges for one of two reasons: it was due to a choice we made, or God chose us to endure the trial for someone else. His ways and thoughts are so much higher than ours, so whatever He leads us to, He will be with us to see us through.

When I was 19, I decided to go into the military. My life was on a downward spiral, but thanks be to God that I had enough sense to do something about my situation before it was too late. I initially wanted to join the Air Force but because I had a year-old son, they wouldn't allow me. He needed to be adopted which normally takes a couple of years. I didn't have that kind of time, so the Army was glad to shuffle me over to their office. They allowed me to give legal guardianship to my mother, which only takes a day to do. I started the process thinking that I was going to be leaving in a matter of months, only to be placed on their deferment list for a year. As I look back, I realize this was a plot and trick of the enemy to get me trapped so I wouldn't break out of the molded environment I was in. I grew up and lived in a neighborhood that was filled with drug dealers, drug addicts, hustlers, and everything else in between and when you're exposed to this and see it daily, you can't help but pick up bad habits through osmosis. You start to evolve with the environment and don't even realize it. This is the path I started to embark upon, and after a few incidents and brushes with death, I knew I had to do something to get away or I wasn't going to live much longer. I did my best to stay out of trouble, keep my nose clean, so I could leave on my intended date. Any mishaps with the law would alter all my plans and I would've been stuck in a matrix designed to destroy me. Finally, the day came for me to start a new life, and on November 3rd, 1993 I left the old, and embraced the new.

I did basic training in Fort Jackson, SC in the brutal cold. Back then you could tell the seasons apart and there were no sunny, warm days around Thanksgiving and Christmas like it is now. We had a holiday break so instead of being finished in the normal 8 weeks, we didn't graduate until February 4, 1994. My next assignment was in Fort Gordon, GA where I studied to be a Telecommunications Specialist. I had scored so high on the ASVAB test that this was the best job they had. It required me to have a Top Security clearance, which set me apart from my peers. I remember a drill sergeant telling me that I stick out like a sore thumb.

I looked at him with a mean look, thinking he was being the ogre we knew him to be during basic training, but he clarified it after he saw my facial expression. He said, "No matter what you do, there is a light about you that you cannot hide. You're different from others and for that reason alone, you will go far in life." He said he saw great things in me, and expected me to succeed in my military plans and career goals.

After five months of AIT (Advanced Individual Training), I learned of my first duty station: Fort Clayton, Panama! I was in shock because I just knew I was going to have what was on my Dream Sheet of duty stations I desired, and overseas was NOWHERE on my list! But when you sign up to serve your country, you go where you are needed…point blank, no questions asked! I left the states in June of 1994, and entered one of the hottest places I had ever experienced. My mother's family is from Ahoskie, NC and if you know anything about the heat in the South, you know that's about as close as you get to feeling how hot Hell is LOL! So here I am, the new kid on the block, or a "newbie" as we're affectionately called. I walked with confidence, I exuded intelligence and I had my head screwed on straight. My body was so fit and muscled from all of the physical training that I turned the heads of men and women, and that brought a lot of unwanted attention. Immediately the advances from men in higher rank started to approach me, but I turned them down with finesse. I had dreams and goals that I wanted to accomplish on my own, and not sleeping my way to the top. They kept trying, and I kept dodging until one day I was cornered. I lived in the barracks which was unisex, but our roommates were the same gender. I had just gotten out of the shower when there was a knock on my door. One of the Lieutenants came looking for my roommate supposedly, but it was a ruse to come on to me. When someone of rank comes in your presence, you must address them and give respect no matter how awkward the situation may be. Here I am half-dressed, waiting for this dude to finish with the dumb questions that I knew was just his way of phishing and trying to feel me out, but I wasn't budging. So, then he pulls rank on me and said that he can make my life easy or hard, my choice. I asked what the hell was that supposed to mean? At this point, the street ways in me was coming out and I knew where he was getting at, so now I'm in defense mode. If he could disrespect me by giving me a sexual ultimatum, then I was going to disrespect him with my answers. At this time my roommate came in, and it startled him so he mumbled something and quickly walked out. I told her what happened, and she warned me that it happens often and to be careful.

Months went by and every now and again I would see the Lieutenant. He would smirk at me, and I would grit on him and roll my eyes. I thought I was good until one night we came back from the NCO club, a hangout spot on the base. I was a bit drunk but not to the point where I was wasted. He was on duty that night, and saw when I went in my room. He knew my roommate was on leave, so he also knew I was alone. He used the master key to come in, put his hand over my mouth, pinned my arms down and raped me. When he finished he said if I told anyone, it would be his word against mine. He told me he could mess my records up, so that I wouldn't advance or worse yet; have me put out of the military with a dishonorable discharge. I didn't know any better, so I believed him. I was working hard on studying for tests and doing what I needed to do to advance and didn't need any setbacks. I told one of my friends the next day what had happened, and her response was, "oh he got you too?" I was in such shock that I just cried uncontrollably, because up to that point I thought I was dreaming. I felt so violated, so yucky inside and no matter how much I showered, I wasn't clean enough. I changed my routine so I could avoid him altogether, and slept with a chair barring the door and a knife under my pillow. There was someone that I had started dating, and we were getting serious but when that happened I broke up with him. I thought he wouldn't believe me, and I didn't think I could be with him sexually since all I did was replay that incident in my mind over and over.

The day came that his tour ended and was being sent to another duty station, undoubtedly to take advantage of someone else. I started feeling at ease and wasn't feeling anxiety all the time, which allowed me to get back to being my normal self. A year had passed by this time, and I resumed going after my next military goals with vigor. I rekindled my relationship with the guy I was seeing, and all seemed to be right in my life. I was in a better head space. I started healing mentally and emotionally and was starting to feel better about life until it happened again. My platoon deployed to Suriname, South America for training, and to oversee the Cubans fleeing the communistic regime of Fidel Castro. I was walking back from my rounds in making sure our communication equipment was intact, when the company sergeant major pulled me into his tent. He was a big, burly guy and was extremely strong and apparently had been drinking. He started fondling me roughly, telling me how much I had turned him on since I got there, and whatever else he could think of. He made me touch his genitals, forcing me to rub him until he became fully erect and pushed my head down to perform oral sex. There was no way I wasn't going to fight back this time, so I tried to scream and push him off, but he was so strong that I was powerless. What seemed like hours was over in a matter of a few seconds after he released himself. He told me to clean myself off before I left out, and he went another way as if nothing happened. I was in such a daze walking back to my tent, wondering how this happened to me again, but this time was worse than the last because of the action that took place. I got so sick to my stomach thinking about it, that I had to be medevac to the unit in Panama. I made up my mind that I wasn't going to take this one, and told the captain of my unit what happened. He was so distraught that it looked like he was fighting tears. The reason was he really liked me as a soldier, my drive and focus and it was his job to protect me and see me succeed. We were also great friends, so it hurt him that I was hurt like that. But the other reason was because he was also friends with the sergeant major, and was very close as they had served in a war together, so this put him in a serious predicament. He told me that he was going to deal with it, when they got back and see to it that I received justice. That never happened. I expected my commander to do his civic duty to me as a soldier in the army, as opposed to salvaging his friendship. Once I saw that I was being given the runaround, I started to feel like I didn't matter, that I was irreplaceable and that what happened to me was an "oh well, deal with it" situation. All of my plans, dreams and goals went up in smoke right before my eyes, and I hated the military and everything it stood for.

I prayed and asked God to give me a way out as my thoughts were starting to be irrational and all over the place. Not even a day later, I found out I was pregnant. To me this was the sign I needed that my prayer was answered. I got out August 20, 2005 with an honorable discharge. If I didn't learn anything else while serving, I learned that honor was everything when being affiliated with the military, so it was imperative that nothing tarnished or stained my name. Even though this was a silver lining, it was also the beginning of a syndrome a lot of ex-military members deal with called PTSD (Post Traumatic Stress Disorder). Back then there wasn't a title nor was it even known, but many were suffering with it. Not only does it cause you to live in fear, anxiety and stress, but you think irrationally and many turn to drugs and alcohol to help cope. I was never a drug person, but alcohol was my weakness, and every chance I got, I drank. From 1995 to 2013 I was clueless that I had this disability, which meant it went untreated all those years, and I grew worse. In this same timeframe, I had 5 more children and the post-partum depression made my condition worse. I couldn't stay gainfully employed, and went from job to job month after month. With no steady income, I became homeless so many times that I lost count. My children had to stay with different family members until I could "get myself together" several times, and once I thought I was on the right track, I fell back into the same cycle. My family thought of me as a screw up, as I couldn't seem to do anything right in their eyes. It's like I could see the disappointment on their faces would turn into words that read, "How did you fall so far from glory?" I never told anyone what happened because I thought no one would believe me, and if they did, what could possibly be done about it after so much time had passed?

I had been praying about my mental issues, and told the Lord that I know something is wrong, but I just don't know what it is. I knew it was stemming from the rapes, but because there was not closure and no justice, it was taking over my life. I asked Him to help me, because I was making really bad choices, and it was causing me and my children to suffer, sometimes so bad that it was unbearable and I wanted to die. But God had other plans, which involved me living and not dying! One day I came across someone at a bus stop that seemed to be an angel in disguise. Somehow, we got on the subject about me being a veteran, and they asked me was I getting any assistance from the military. I said I didn't know I was entitled to anything, and they told me to try because you never know. They stated they knew someone who was receiving disability for sinus issues and another for acne so surely, I could think of an ailment that I could get paid for LOL. I thought about, and decided to pursue. After all, what was the worst that could happen besides being told no, right? I went to a local Veteran Affairs office to talk to someone about what I could receive, and while standing in line my eyes were drawn to a poster that read three words that ultimately changed my life: Military Sexual Trauma. It proceeded to say that the military recognizes this has occurred throughout the years, and they want to make things right. I felt an excitement rise in me that I hadn't felt in years! I knew right then and there that God answered my prayers, and He was going to justify the wrongs His way.

What made you decide to start the business that you're in?
Life changed drastically for me. I received much needed therapy, disability compensation along with medical benefits. I was able to go back to school at the government's expense; not only me but my children as well. It ignited a passion inside of me to help others just like me, so I started a consulting business with an emphasis in commercial construction. I want to obtain commercial and government contracts and in turn employ veterans with and without disabilities. I understood what it's like to feel like you've been robbed of a golden opportunity to live a good life, and have financial freedom, so my goal is to find lucrative opportunities that pay well and help pave the way for all to live their dreams.

What made you LEAP? How did you make the leap from a secure paid job to starting your own business?

I am pretty independent and have had to rely on myself often, but I recognize the fact that we aren't to do all things alone, so oftentimes I have to solicit the help of others. My natural family and church family help me out a lot, and I in turn make sure that I return the favor. This is the only way I can balance out my responsibilities so that I'm not overwhelmed. This project and business model has been four years in the making, so naturally there were so many times that I wanted to quit and give up, because it looked as if my dreams weren't going to manifest. I even walked away from it and counted myself as average, thinking it wasn't meant for me to be an entrepreneur but as soon as I threw in the towel, God threw it back and said, "Get back in the fight. You don't quit until I tell you to!" When I look at my children, when I look at how others live a lavish life, when I see all that I have overcome by the grace of God...THAT keeps me going! I am so determined to succeed, that I refuse to stop. As P. Diddy would say, "can't stop, won't stop!"

What was the best advice you ever received? Worst advice?

The best advice I've ever received was that I can be whatever I chose to be, and that if I believe it, then I will certainly achieve it. The worst advice I heard but refused to receive, was that because of my lack of construction experience, I should just find something else along the lines of what I've done while working in the corporate world. I really knew that they were saying because I'm a black woman, I have no place in this good old' boy's world. All that does is add more fuel to the fire of my passion, propelling me to make sure I make it.

We All know the saying It takes a village to raise a child, but for a mom starting her own business, the village may be a state. So who do you turn to or go to for help? Who are your go-to people/services?

I had to go to a lot of women business networking events, and I also sought the help of SBA or Small Business Administration. They had a chock full of knowledge, a website with tons of resources and the people ready to answer any questions that I had.

What do you do to unwind and recharge? How important is this for a Mompreneur?

It is extremely important to take some time out for yourself, especially after dealing with the stress of taking care of your family and also running a business. Once you see that you are running on fumes, or your attitude is off the rails towards people, that is a sign that you need to go somewhere to decompress and to recharge. If you are fortunate enough to leave out of the state and go somewhere else for a complete change of scenery, then do it! But if you are not, at least get out of the house or even get out of the city and go somewhere else for a small and slight vacation. This will do wonders for you when you come back to face whatever situations you left open.

What book would you recommend for a Mompreneur just starting out? Why this particular one?

I would advise women to get Dr. Stacia Pierce's The Success Journal. You can literally change and transform your life not just with this journal but any journal. When you find that what is written is real, you can change the course of your life. Of course there are many other books to read but for someone that is starting out and you want to see your life go a certain way, get a journal and write it how you wanted to go.

What are some of the ways that you involve or have involved your family in your business?

I have often asked my thirteen-year-old to help me with business as my assistant. He helps me, he prays for me, he encourages me, he compliments me often and he always tells me that I am going to make it big. With this type of positivity around me, it is easy to ask not only for assistance but for him to just be around. He makes me feel as if I can accomplish anything.

What did it feel like to make your first dollar as a Mompreneur? How long did that take?

I have been in business for about two years as a name, but someone decided to take a chance on me. As a minority business, I helped him but he also helped me to get what is called past performance in the construction industry. It was a small contract that I was excited about worth $5,000. I treated it as if it were $5,000,000! I know that day is coming soon so what you are grateful and appreciative for on a small scale will undoubtedly manifest on a larger scale.

Kids & Significant others, do and say the darndest things. Please share with us one of your funniest moments, embarrassing moments, saddest moments, and most rewarding moment that involving your family and your business?

One of the most embarrassing yet eye opening moments was when my now 21 year old daughter was around 8 or 9. I was financially struggling so much that I often had to pawn items for food or gas. This meant precious items that were of value to both me and my children. I can't quite remember what the item was, but as usual my oldest son noticed it missing. He asked me about it, and I was honest about pawning it. He was saddened by it and did his best to hide his feelings, but not her. She blurted out, "You keep pawning everything and we're not gonna have anything left. You're probably gonna pawn us next!" I could not believe it and I wanted to whip her, but she was right. I never forgot what she said as that was my motivation to get things together. My financial issues are not my children's fault.

What is Your Favorite Quote?

"You must have a RIGHTEOUS INDIGNATION" to want to be wealthy and rich, otherwise you will always remain the same!" Dr. Stacia Pierce

Leave us with ONE word to describe a Mompreneur.

DETERMINED!

A Woman's Worth Bio

I first want to thank Abba, my Heavenly Father, for allowing me to be a part of this amazing opportunity. Without you Lord, and without your grace, where would I be? I dedicate this book to my six heartbeats, Dachon (24) A'Chanti (21) Stefon (18) Marreon (13) Yoshua (8) and Israel (6). Thank you for being my daily motivation. I told you it wasn't going to always be like this. Watch how life as we know is going to change right before our very eyes! We Made It!!

Marqueta Plum Jenkins is the mot her to six children. Their ages are from 24 to 6. They are her "why" and what makes her continue to strive for success. She currently lives in Norfolk, VA and attends Kingdom Gates International Ministries in Virginia Beach, VA. She can be contacted by the way, at the following:

Facebook: Marqueta Plum Jenkins
Instagram: billionaire_boss_lady
Twitter: TheMakedaGroup

CHAPTER 13

MARY HAZWARD FERNANDEZ

Mary Kay IND Sales Director/CEO WOHI

Who is the Mompreneur behind the business? Tell us about you.

WHO I AM STARTS WITH where I come from. I was a little girl who loved to draw pictures in the dirt back when dirt pies were the norm and children would play in the dirt and pretend to cook dinner. My creativeness led me to drawing faces. As I grew older I drew all kinds of faces and hairstyles. A lot of people would comment on my drawing ability

I got real comfortable with my desire to help others by creating events to support whatever organization I was in. People would describe me as very enthusiastic, creative and organized happy person. In High school, my teacher allowed me to work independent of the class, doing my own thing. To further express myself, I danced in the modern dance group and went on to become Head Majorette.

Watching my Dad as an engineer at the shipyard made me want to become an engineer also. So off I went to a nearby college in pursuit of my Engineering career. College became another place to become creative and involved so off we went getting involved and creative. It was about that time that I got involved with my community civic league watching my Dad and watching my mom produce Building Fun Fashion shows for church in my child hood church home.

Being a mompreneur, allowed me to serve and volunteer and touch lives. I loved being a part of the PTA and in my community it was the business association and the community civic league. My end goal was help wherever I could.

There was always a desire to pay it forward and express my gratitude to God for taking care of my children and husband and me, so I constantly found myself creating programs to serve others. One is a Mentoring Circle for The Portsmouth Drug Co submitted my proposal to mentor clients of the legal system, which was approved by the Judge. The mission is to impact the way the clients think and create some new options for handling personal decisions and negative influencers. This has been over 9-12 years volunteering. My cup is full and it pours out in gratitude by serving others.

Some call me an encourager, motivator, mentor and Coach. I love all those descriptions.

My brother called me a Rock of Support and Leadership and my Sister Betty calls me capable blessed and highly favored.

I keep the enriching descriptions and don't count the negative nor give them any value. It is so key to staying positive and staying the course. Weigh what you listen to by the how you value the speaker.

All of us have some not so nice people along our path. Remember ... Keep it moving.

My father in heaven calls me more than a conqueror and with all the above I believe I can do all things.

What made you decide to start the business that you're in?
With the highs and lows of the economy, I continued to adjust to changes in customer needs and buying habits. I noticed that several of my customers were young teachers when I met them and had moved on to become principles and some were called into the ministry and were growing on their journey. Some retired and bought the coach life and some took on grandchildren.

Many of my customers would speak of someday; I'd like to do this or that. As the years went by I noticed that they had not acted on those goals and dreams. I noticed that the great job titles and wonderful life accomplishments did not make it easier for them to jump, move, take action or get started on their personal deep-felt goals kind of out the box goals, like starting a business. Not to mention that some actually did jump from those 9-5 and began their businesses.

So, I set up my new parent company as an effort to do more projects that would impact a larger group of people, you see not everyone wants to do what you do but the leadership and mentoring skills were transferrable.

So, watching many women letting the clock tick without encouragement to act on those dreams and realizing we are daily getting older.... birthed my flood of emotions that made me feel like I must do something to make a tangible difference in women's lives... and what came forth was Women of Help and Influence (WOHI) and The WOHI COACH.

I believed that every woman can be a woman of Help and Influence by sharing their gifts and talents. Then put them in the form of a business or service that the next woman would be impacted by. I felt that if talented and gifted women could share their skills and wisdom that they could influence another generation of women and each other.

One painful memory on my journey was a young woman with one little girl. I would see her at workshops and events. We'd smile and say hello. That young mompreneur committed suicide. I did not know if I wanted to put this story in the book, but it is to say that we never know how our lives can touch another life if we reach out. This young woman did not look like the pain that she must have been living, but a network of women mentoring women and encouraging and empowering or equipping one another could change a life and even save a life.

WOHI aims to move women forward by connecting people services and opportunities. We create customized, strategic plans specific for each client to run their goal to touch down. To start the process, we created "THE WOHI's" our Private Facebook group of likeminded women mostly 40+. A great place to grow, share and collaborate. Every client is different and may need a mild, medium or intensive plan of action.

Let's Skip to Evening College, the twins are about 8 or 9 about now. Working full time days and going to school at night to finish up my B.S. Degree in Electronics Technology. My sanctuary was home and in public I was like a Mama Bear, very protective of my business and mechanical about projects of any type. I was a woman on a mission.

I had had enough of that SHY BOX or Glass Prison as some would call it. To set my set free, the decision was made in my heart to put myself out there with projects, clubs or organizations that would require me to speak or engage people. The group of choice was the EVENING COLLEGE STUDENT GOVERNMENT. The mentors were great and became longtime friends and my fellow organization members were all admirable individuals. One of the projects was producing and directing fashions shows that we used as fundraisers. We needed the student models to be able to put on their own make up on and look professional. What came to mind? Mary Kay Cosmetics. They taught their customers how to do just what we needed. Truly all things work together for the good because the Professional Beauty Consultant who worked with the students would someday become my personal sponsor into Mary Kay.

A few years went by and now I am in my Home and married to my best friend Jose who happens to be out to sea at the time. My Skin was desperately dry and my hands were full of chalices so bad that they would scratch my face if I was not careful. I needed me some MARY KAY. I knew it would work. I sought it out and it was what I called too expensive so I let my hands and face make do with all kinds of lotions and products that did not do the job. But I surely was not going to spend $52 on my face. That was the cost of the Basic Skin Care Set.

Low and behold a few months later I found someone who could give me a facial and I booked a class for someone else. At the same time, my friend down the street was hosting a MK Party so I canceled that party I was to hold since we shared some of the same friends. At my neighbor's party the question was asked, "WHO DO YOU KNOW WHO YOU THINK WOULD BE GOOD AT DOING WHAT I DO?" I was told that the reply was in unison, Mary Down the street, she is one busy lady, she volunteers, goes to school helps with this and that…she would be great. THAT WAS a huge blessing being referred to this beauty consultant… who turned out to be the very same consultant from my Evening College adventure.

She invited me to a guest event breakfast that up and coming Saturday. She said leave the husband and kids at home and treat yourself to some girl time. In my mind, I began to think, everyone in my home had something going on, School activities, husband had baseball and I had school, work and housework…I leaped at the chance.

Now if you have time, let me tell you about that breakfast and what happened next. I arrived on the second floor of a downtown Norfolk hotel. The women were warm and welcoming. I was not use to that. I went to the guest class where they explained how the company works and I had my facial.

The facts made since to this engineering mind…I began to think of all the things I could do for my family sooner than later if I had that kind of freedom and flexibility… When she asked Is there anyone who would like to begin their MK Career, Blah Blah and Blah because I did not hear another word, I was quick to say I DO!!! And the dreams began. And I had no idea how that decision would more than change the course of my life!!!!!!!! I was a woman on a mission!!!!

What made you LEAP? How did you make the leap from a secure paid job to starting your own business?

Tough times demanded that tough decisions be made. Downsizing was the new word on the horizon. Big stable companies that I would have never thought would lay people off or down size, were doing just that. IBM for one made the news and headlines. Shortly the rumors began that GE was downsizing and  eventually would close. This large company that hired so many in neighboring cities where so many of us had bought our first homes with and had children in school and some had children in college now had many fearful of losing one of the best jobs with all those great benefits. I had a 1-year old, a 5-year-old and twins approaching their early teens.

Looking back at the twin's life at the age of barely walking. My mind drifted back to a typical morning of getting them ready and me to work on time by 6am for the 6 -2 Shift. This is how it looked. I am and showering by 3:30 Am., next I get the twins up at 4 am. (Now in my head is my Bosses voice. Mary, you'll need to be sick dead or dying to miss another day.) You see I had begun my MK Career and I was moving fast from start to Red Jacket in about 45 days so I could attend a Directors MTGs and Career Conference and on to debuting as a Sales Director my first year so I could earn all the income avenues to meet my family expenses and goals. I took off approximately 3 days a month on the regular until my boss called me into the office to say I must penalize you and give you this warning. You can't do that. I said, I thought you could be absent 3 times a month and he said no, its three times max in a quarter. I was already a sales Director by this time.

It was so foggy this one morning that my dear nephew had to sit on the hood of my car so we could stay straight because we could only see about 2 feet in front of us. We made it to the baby sitter and off I flew to work short of a speeding ticket.

I risked getting fired to get my business up and running and thank God, I did. The pink slips and Layoff packages meeting were going on almost every day. By the grace of God my engineering division was one of the last to leave only a hand full of us were left working in this huge ghost town like production plant.

With the memories of those mornings of fog and 3am and speeding to work….I felt in my heart that I did not want to go thru that again. I thought Lord No Job would justify the baby sitter cost, the time away from the children and being alone while husband out to sea.

I planned and played with number scenarios and decided that if I worked my MK Career and held my appointments and took care of my customers that I could make enough to pay bills and add to my husband's income. I prayed and began to feel confident that I could really do this. I built up my courage and prepared my talk for when my husband would call from overseas. Our Talk went something like this. Baby, I think I can work MK Full time. This would save us on sitters and I can be a working stay at home mom. So what do you think? HE said, OK. If that's what you want to do.

I said yes, and He said ok. When the GE doors closed I took the leap. (I made sure I was busy and not wasting time. I stayed engaged with people by substitute teaching and continuing to volunteer in the business and neighborhood organizations. Full-time mompreneur. There is just no telling what a woman on a mission can do.

I was the only Work from home mom for blocks. I would walk my children to the bus stop along with about 10 other little ones. I had a chance to be PTA mom and band mom not only for my children, but for a few others who asked me, "Are you coming to college with us Ms. Fernandez." I would have if they had a place for me.

How do you balance or how did you balance your work/home life?
Balancing or juggling life home and work at different stages of the Momprenuer Journey takes shifting from situation to situation much like a ROLLER DERBY skater mission possible. KEEP IT MOVING! That's why Nemo is my MK unit Mascot. KEEP ON SWIMMING or KEEP IT MOVING!!

During the first few months of being an entrepreneur, where it was me the Twins and Hubby, nicknamed "B" Poppy D" and Jr, we had a fire that made us homeless if it were not for my parents who let us live with them while the insurance company renovated our home. The twins were in school and I was called at work about the fire. That same night of the fire, I had a MK Class Scheduled. I was grateful everyone was fine, so to praise GOD and to keep things normal I got the children settled and I held that appointment with black smoke in my nails and the smell of smoke in my clothes. Remember, keep it moving.

Starting out in My Mk Career I had what I call "No MONEY SENSE" that means I was winging it on money decisions and I came up with this great formula...I get a paycheck a week so I can have a bill a week. Good idea. Not in the long run.

When the children were little we had a great routine. My Shift moved from 6-2 to 9-5 now that I had been promoted to Electronics Technician. I would get off work at 5, go to make my copies and plan my business development weekly live meetings call Monday Live held one night a week!! Soon as I got home it was all family time, dinner, school stories and a bit of TV. The older teens would watch the baby girl this was before my son was born and a bit of the time after. The twins grew up. Don't get me started on the teen years of each of my children. All the amazing things of growing up.

Our Family loved being together so, if Husband was out to sea, I kept the children entertained and worked my MK around their lives and when I had to go for a 24 hour or 3-day business trip, my husband would watch the children.

Skip now to the sandwich years of our lives. That's when you have young children and caring for elderly parents. My parents were elderly and most to all of my siblings lived out of town. Over a period of 10 years I now call my PINK CADILLAC YEARS, I had the honor of assisting my Father with the last days of my brother, then years of caring for my mother with my Dad until Mom Passed away, then my Oldest Brother passing then on to a few years of enjoying my Fathers as he creeped into dementia and Alzheimer's. My ALL IN ONE real Sister was like a mother and sister and the best of friends. Betty was right by my side mentally and emotionally from her home state encouraging me and supporting us though the process. She stood out like no other as an anchor to share tears, fears and guidance.

I call them my Cadillac years, because while others were building Pink Car Units my head was in the home game and enjoying my assignment that my mom told me early in my career...TAKE YOUR FAMILY WITH YOU on this journey. That meant make sure you keep your priorities in order.

A typical day for many years went like this. After my son would drive himself to school. Dad and I would go to breakfast every morning Monday thru Friday. HE would pull up in his car and I was ready to go. We did this until I had to take the keys and start driving us. We ate at every restaurant possible. It made him so proud that he was with his daughter and as we looked around. It was a lot of his elderly buddies sitting alone with their coffee and newspaper. Being able to assist my Dad was to me like winning a Cadillac. I have those treasured memories. Dad would make sure Saturday and Sunday were left for family time. Each night at dinner I would make sure to fix him a great dinner plate every day! We maximized every day.

Keeping priorities of God Family and Career, I kept my family close to us as possible. Every year that there was a Career conference within 3-4 hours away. My Whole family would go. I went to class and family enjoyed the hotel and amenities until I was free then it was ON FAMILY TIME. My dearest memory was when my husband wrote me this great letter where he said he used to love the Navy but he loves being with us more. Mary Kay Changed the way we lived our lives. Owning your own business makes you the boss and the Scheduler.

I must mention, Life continues to happen despite your goals, bills and dreams are. When Dad died, I was equipped by him to handle the business of death as he called it, but Grief will have its way...it creeped in on me after a couple of years I woke up and realized that I was moving in slow motion, paying every bill slow, 3 months late, not opening mail; and only by the grace of God did we not go under. I thanked my Husband for Standing by my side. I thank God for the desire to stand strong for my MK Unit and keep providing Training, and support to them and my customers. Being my own boss had a lot to do with our financial recovery that took some years to restore. I got to working double time.

What do you say to yourself when you feel like giving up? What keeps you going?

Here is one realization. Our parents had nice china dishes and keep sakes they loved and passed on to us. As years went on I noticed many children of younger generations did not value or care about things that same way.

Second I noticed that, our parents' generation had children to care for them and support their journey in their older ages. We don't know what the future holds so I am reminded daily that I want to do all I can to prepare financially for my future and the retirement years that I want to spend with my husband on a beach somewhere.

I remind myself that every day is a good day when you get to wake up. I start thanking God from the moment I am conscious in the morning because I now some were not able to get up. Stay connected to your why. Know that your why will evolve with age and time.

I take God's word and promises as guidepost to keep me moving forward.

When I look around and see how people were and are aging, I remind myself that God said our latter days would be better than our former days.

So, when I found my body acting like the sciatic nerve was ruling about 15 years ago...I went thru the process of physical therapy. For 5 Years, I went back for my back pain, my leg pain, my hip pain then repeats the cycle...I finally asked the physical therapist what is the root cause so that we can address this. She gave me charts and great explanation and then I said so, the body is going to age but if I make this lifestyle change such as lower my high heels, stay in exercise and stretch mode and reduce my weight that I could keep it at bay long as possible or even wipe it out. I said on it... So, telling myself and believing that life on earth was to be as it is in heaven, then this situation must come under my feet and the authority of God's word, I am grateful to be walking and able to get out of bed just like that, instead of taking one hour of moving thru pain to sit up, then put my feet on the floor. I am grateful.

I love people and people will be people so when I find myself in situations where some of those people walk away or are cruel, dishonest or mean, in earlier days I was shocked and amazed and deeply hurt. My daughter taught me "Mom, don't be shocked and amazed by anyone." She noticed it grieved my heart and deeply hurt me" She then taught me as the wonderful young adults all my children have become and blessed me with their wisdom. She taught me to get over it!! Let it go. Remember who it is coming from and reset my heart and move on. Learn from the past and don't allow negative people a place in your heart. So, I learned to love al people but not to let all people into the sacred place in your heart. Now I can keep it moving working to be me doing all the good that I can to all the people that I can and to Keep God First, Family Second and Career Third. I remind myself that the JOY of the Lord is my strength, so do the things that make me happy.

Yes, I do cry off the hurts and disappointments to let out the toxins. I enjoy family time and work in my flowerbed. Whatever brings you joy...Make sure you do those things. They are like medicine to the bones.

What was the best advice you ever received? Worst advice?
The best Advice is also the WORST advice in this case and that was

"Stand in line and wait your turn. Stay in Position Your Turn will come."

This was good advice that serves me to this day, when it meant don't quit stay the course.

Your turn is coming.

That was good advice if you are in a 9-5 job system where you must prove yourself in the promotional opportunity zone. For an entrepreneur, it does not mean the same thing and nor does it work the same way. Sometimes this rule does not apply because the rule of the game is so different. You must first remember you are the boss and must decide what you want, how quickly do you want it and how to work the plan to attain it, it being your end goal.

When you are an independent contractor, it means just that. Now, if getting the marketing plan includes team building to get to the next level and ultimately to the level you dream of then it is very important to be a team player and to lead by example. Learn the process and give as much as you take.

No waiting in line that line is invisible and does not exist. Learn the process and work the process.

What I learned is that if you wait, time keeps moving and people and mentors and love ones are steady moving up and on. I am so grateful for my amazing MK Mentors and the company support system. You are never alone from mentor to staff.

How is this super GOOD ADVICE? It is super good if you come in with an end in mind. Trusting the process means also that we must grow and learn the business. I truly was not as confident, peaceful steady and a professional business developer and mentor when I started that I have grown to be today.

When I did my first MK Facial I put step two on before the first step and they looked kind of funny but I kept going and the class was a great success. That good advice made me stay the course and stay on the path of learning from some of the most amazing MK Mentors in the world and they loved us mentored us in their own unique ways. I kept on growing myself and my skills and my confidence to come to the conclusion that they were passing the torch I learned that I can impact a lot of women's lives who have no idea how meaningful and rewarding owning your own business can be.

Wait your turn. It does not matter how fast others around you are moving. Focus on your Goal. Work your Plan. Maximize your Gifts. Be yourself. Your Time is coming. That Good advice standing strong. How in the world did I end up experiencing writing a book a huge dream of mine? OMG, I remained hungry to learn all I could about helping others achieve their goal. I stayed in Workshops and events to sharpen my skill and at one of those amazing workshops. This Lioness of a WOMAN, Earthy real and full of good information! Taught my class. I was in position to Learn and I am so grateful I stayed the course, kept my focus and stood in LIFE'S LINE and Met Lioness Latrece Williams McKnight. She says with passion and purpose. You can do this what are you waiting for. WOW! Full Circle.

We All know the saying It takes a village to raise a child, but for a mom starting her own business, the village may be a state. So who do you turn to or go to for help? Who are your go-to people/services?
Truly it does take a village to raise a Child. My parents were the grounding influence for the years they were living. Mom Frances echoed values of a lady, and to always keep yourself clean and have clean underwear on, and comb your hair and look nice. She received her last college

degree at age 70. Dad, imparted strong work ethics and calm. He led by example. He loved to cook for us. He loved my mother and us to the utmost. Both Dad and Mom loved education and read tons of books and loved having their grandchildren around especially for bid family Christmas and Thanksgiving Dinners teaching by example, that family is important.

When my sister passed our rock of support was extended family. We made my sister's family a part of our family and the amazing Speights family was added to our lives like a second Mother and Father and more sisters and brothers. School and extra activities, band and the arts filled the rest of the gaps. Church and Sunday school was so key as the children were young and as they grew they began to make their worship and spiritual choices for themselves.

What do you do to unwind and recharge? How important is this for a Mompreneur?

To unwind and recharge is key to keeping your sanity and health. To unwind, I taught myself to have an on and off switch. It is important to not work 24/7 even if we wear all the hats of the business. In the younger years, after the children are set and their needs were met I made some me time. I have a few ways to recharge my mind and energy. One was Playtime. I enjoy being with my children so we would regularly make time to go to the park, or walk the Portsmouth water front or go to the beach and on Sunday night we'd get ice cream and look at America's Funniest Video. My husband and I still meet at 7 to look at AFV when possible. Another way to recharge and renew is a warm bubble bath in my mental retreat space, My bathroom, for a couple of hours. Pamper time. A few times when my husband would see that I was wired or had had a long day...he would run the warm bath and that was my signal...time to cut off the day and take care of myself. Oddly enough, it totally refreshes and renews me by working in my yard, cutting the grass, creating flower beds. This is like heaven I can start in the am and take breaks and go back and end at sundown. I may be stiff the next day but I love working in my yard playing with dirt kind of.

What book would you recommend for a Mompreneur just starting out? Why this particular one?

Recommending one book is very hard because there are so many authors who have molded my thinking. So, I would start with "Woman Thou Art Loosed" by T.D. Jakes. This book was a cleansing of the soul. It reached deep and pulled out things that were in my mind that freed me to let go and let

What are some of the ways that you involve or have involved your family in your business?

My husband the encourager would give me a new scripture each year unconsciously or consciously that I would put on my mirror or wall. Jose and the children have put labels on product and help me load and unload the car. My son became my computer expert starting at age 10 He encourage me to get my first computer because as he put it, it is the way of the future. (AT 10) In later years he helped with music as DJ for events. My daughters have helped with the teaching me to use the new smartphones and apps on the computer to being on event programs and welcome team. My family has supported every event possible especially our Annual Stars Reds and Achievers Luncheon Cruise for families and friends. They are the best and help in so many ways that makes this a family business.

What did it feel like to make your first dollar as a Mompreneur? How long did that take?

It took me approximately 3 months to make a profit. When I made my first dollar, I felt so proud of myself and excited that I could really impact my family and teach others how to do the same. Using a strategy called the Star Consultant Quarterly contest that runs every 3 months, I was able to take a profit or write myself a paycheck. This worked when I would use the disciplines and work strategies taught to me by my mentor and mapped out by this contest. The lesson here was you do not spend every penny you make.

Kids & Significant others, do and say the darndest things. Please share with us one of your funniest moments, embarrassing moments, saddest moments, and most rewarding moment that involving your family and your business?

Besides that beautiful letter my husband wrote me while out to sea. My Son came home from school one day at age 7 or 8 and said. "Ma, I am proud of you and Da. " I asked him why Honey. He responded, "You work and keep the lights on and food for us." I hugged him and thought to myself, that he must have seen or heard something while at school that touched his heart.

What is Your Favorite Quote?

I can do all things though the Lord Jesus Christ Which Strengthens me. (In fear, in doubt, in despair, in joy, in any situation I lean on this work)

Leave us with ONE word to describe a Mompreneur.

Resilient

A Woman's Worth Bio

Mary Hazward Fernandez was born and raised in the city of Portsmouth, VA to the parents Johnson and Mary Hazward. She is one of 10 children. Mary is married to Jose and has 5 wonderful children.

Mary attended Mount Hermon Elementary school just walking distance from her home. Mary Loved drawing faces with makeup and fun hair do's and fashions. This lead her to sewing by hand and creating clothes she loved until her parents bought her first sewing machine.

Mary fell in love with music in middle school playing the violins and modern dancing in high school where she became head Majorette n the Marching band- THE NORCOM GREYHOUNDS Marching Band!

Mary went on to college taking courses at TCC and ODU and graduated from Norfolk State University with a B.S. Degree in Electronic Technology. She took on employment at General Electric TV Plant where she was promoted to Engineering Department after several years of working other positions in GE.

Mary became very active in her community developing activities for the youth that would encourage their leadership and confidence. Later Mary began her Direct Sales Business with a fortune 500 Company and invested her time in the Business community associations.

With her love to serve others Mary Created programs and workshops that included a Mentoring Program for the Drug Court Program where she conducts a mentoring circle for men and women once a month for over 9 years. After years of mentoring women and creating projects and events Mary began her DBA. Women of Help and Influence where her goal is to support women in their quest for personal and business development as they start-up and launch their Businesses and goals. These two-business work very well together fulfilling her goals to impact the lives of women and their families.

CHAPTER 14

EDWINA V. WILSON

CEO/Founder At Kelly's Choice, Inc.

Who is the Mompreneur behind the business? Tell us about you.

I, EDWINA V. WILSON, AM built for life's journey. I'm a wife to my loving husband Quarry Wilson whom I adore and love so much. I am a mother to 4 young adults, 3 daughters and 1 son. They are now 33, 31, 27 & 26 years young. My 31yr old was diagnosed with cerebral palsy and other disabilities after birth. When she was 3 months, concerned about her development, I took her to get looked at. It was then I found out that my baby was not like other babies. She had seizures at birth, a stroke on her right side, and amblyopic which is a lazy eye and low and behold, "your child will have disabilities growing up. I didn't know what or how to feel. Hmm I thought, well no, since there's no guarantee, I'll accept her just as God created her to be, after all she was blue due to lack of oxygen at delivery she was not breathing for about 20 mins, doctors wanted to give up on her after 3 mins but thank God for her aunt who was in the back while they try to bring Kelly to life, she's here today because she wouldn't let them give up on her and God had a greater plan. Had they not sent me home 3 different times we would probably have a different story. So I said, no I'm going to love her, groom her, mold her and raise her just the way she is and here we go 31 years later. She needs total care and I have been providing care to her for 31 years now and it truly hasn't all been easy. If I tell you that I didn't want to give up sometimes, I would be telling you a story. It got hard and difficult sometimes and I didn't see life because as a baby, all I saw was a cute little precious baby girl that needed a lot of love and care but I didn't see the future, a lot of love, care and attention for the long haul. But her smile, her love, her caring and her being my child with Gods strength to carry on my strength grew and I continued the journey. And a grandmother to 4 absolutely beautiful granddaughters which I love so dearly. My oldest granddaughter graduated this year and I'm so proud of her. She's driving, has her own car, working and getting ready to start college in August 2017. I'm so blessed to have such an awesome family. With my strong faith in God and will power to not limit Kelly, she has thrived high above the doctor's expectations. I didn't see no other way but allow her to be like her siblings.

I was born and raised in Prince George County, Maryland in the city of Landover. I graduated from Largo High in Upper Marlboro. Both my parents are living. I have one brother and one living sister. My oldest sister who is deceased (1994) was my sister and best friend. I felt like I lost everything when she passed. She was that person that would always be there for me when I was going through while in my first marriage. She would sit on the phone when I called knowing it was me when the other line was silent. I loved that about her; she didn't judge me but would often remind me that I didn't have to be in that situation. It was heart breaking to have lost her.

I am one that never gives up; I pray and fight my way through everything. At least I thought it was me but I later realized as the struggles, challenges, hardships, loses, domestic violence, homelessness etc. continued throughout my adult life that it wasn't me, it was God all along that has been keeping me through it all. Growing up my life was peaches and cream, I wanted for nothing in THINGS...but I realized that love wasn't always there like parents should show their children. Or should I say, they showed it in all the wrong ways and that was by giving. As I got older I started to realize that my father was so much like his stepfather, mean (that raised him along with his mother) and my mother was like her mother, they just didn't know how to say, I love you, give hugs or even just a kiss on the forehead if nothing else. My thoughts were to make sure I raise my kids different and that's what I did, all about loving one another. Even before getting off the phone or leaving for the day.

My life hasn't always been easy as an adult. I was married in 1984 at the young age of 18. I had my first daughter right after High School. I met him when I was in the 8th grade. I moved to Norfolk in Dec 1984 right out of high school and my father was very upset, which truly surprised me because I honestly didn't think he cared. However, living in a whole different state and him being in the military, things didn't go so well. It was a lot of cheating going on that really wasn't very healthy for the family. Then things got ugly after years of being together, into an abusive, physical and verbal relationship. I found myself wondering sometimes what was I doing there for so long and having 2 more kids after the fact. Shipping through some years when I had my son I knew it was time to break away. My life and my son's life could have ended while in delivery because I started hemorrhaging and the placenta started pulling away from the wall, an emergency C-section had to be done to save us. My son or I could die but God had a different plan. I was told that Red Cross called my husband at the time but he didn't want to come in. That was that door that was open for me to walk away. To soon find out that he was seeing someone on the ship. Ok, I see! I lost all desires when Red Cross told me that, I mean what did I have to hang in there for. After all he opted out. So here I am with an 11month old infant, Kelly, who can't do for herself, and my oldest. My sister came down and then my mother came to help for a bit. I ended up buying a double stroller. I had Kelly in the back, with my 11mos in front of her and my infant in the front seat and my oldest alongside of us. The struggle was real. This is another reason why I'm a Mompreneur and great Mother.

When I was told that my husband didn't want to fly in, I knew then that God answered my prayers because I didn't know how to leave, but he opened a door for me to walk away. Years of torture, heart ache and pain even while separated and divorce, I ran from him for years of moving so many times. I went into a depression and suffered from major migraines and was at the hospital so many times. I remember several times when he knew I was alone he would come over all nice and I would open the door and all he wanted was one thing. When I would refuse he would start with the verbal put downs. This one time he cut the cords to my house phone, caller id and iron cord. I went to the command and of course he wasn't happy about that but I was tired of being treated like anything because you were mad. Times when it was the two oldest we would go to Maryland to visit, he would drop me and the girls off at my parents' house and he would go over near the mall where I lived and see this girl. Yep I found out that it was the same girl that he was seeing or liked before I met him. By the way we met when I was in the 8th grade and he was in the 9th grade, he was a new student at the school and I just happen to be working guidance and the library and was the one to take him around to his classes. This chocolate, short and bald headed cute  thang. Little did I know. But it was all good at one point. I would often say, I'm not angel and I have made many mistakes and bad choices but I truly didn't deserve to go through what I did. I mean it started early in our marriage. I remember when Kelly was born a year later he got another person pregnant while he was in Norfolk at his youngest brothers graduation, hmm no wonder you wouldn't answer the phone or call me back. Then the girl he was seeing on the ship, she got pregnant. I mean stuff. Loads of abuse, too much to mention. He had a nerve to get mad at me when he came home from sea but all along he had plans to move with this chic. I was working at Granby High as a secretary which soon ended because dude sent his father to come get me from work one day while he moved some of our stuff from the house for him and this chic. I was totally pissed because you take away from the kids to have for someone else, now that was ridiculous. It never ended (meaning the constant coming to my house or following me) until I decided to leave Virginia after my kids got out of school in 1997 and move back to Maryland. When living in Maryland, I was working at EPA, I met some really great people, I became friends with 3 ladies and we would always take lunch at the same time. We went out to happy hours one day after work. They would ask me quite often but most often I would not because of my husband. The one time I did go, I told him. The minute I walked in the door, he was waiting. He snatched me up, punched me and pushed me onto the table. We fought some kind of bad that day. I got a chance to call my mother and she and my sister came to get me and the girls. I stayed away for a couple of days but he was so good at telling me how he would change, so eventually I went back.

The first time I became homeless was when the rent wasn't being paid by my ex and we got evicted. I had no idea he wasn't paying the rent until I came home and an eviction notice was on the door. I struggled to find a place and it wasn't easy or quick enough. We went through some things. I was asking people if we could stay there for a while until I find an apartment.

Then I was living in Maryland and after 911 the company I was working at in Springfield decided to close that office and go back to their corporate office in PA. My job ended in November. We got severance, but that just wasn't enough especially when Quarry's job then slowed down. We were back at not enough to pay rent for the next month. I couldn't find a job quick enough and we ended up having to move because the owner took us to court.

We were everywhere trying to live. I was talked about, lied on, humiliated and cursed at. But God just kept on keeping me humble. A friend ended up having her cousin move in with her while we stayed at her cousin's house. We did that for about 3 months but we could not find a job. So we had to leave. When I say, we were everywhere, I mean we were everywhere. Up and down the road, here and there and everywhere. Bless my kid's heart. The last place they ended up was at my father's house, he didn't want me there, I cried because after 40 something years, my father has never done that to me. I always had a key to his house and was always welcomed but something went wrong. I ended up sleeping in my car, the car that I got when no one else would finance me. My credit was jacked up, smacked up and some but I drove of that lot with the car I wanted with no money down. Only God, he was looking after me and I didn't even realize it. That car was everything to me when I end up living out of it while my kids were at my father's house. I would ride the beltway looking for spots to stay every night. Some nights, I cried and some nights and days a tear wouldn't come out. But God kept me covered every night.

Finally I heard about an organization that would help you out if you have someone in your family with a disability. I went to them and they gave me 1st months' rent and deposit once I found a place. Wow, the streets had ended. We got the 4 bedroom townhouse and life went on. I end up starting a government contracting business right before we moved and my first month we made over $3,000 and every month it got better. I started with nothing but a few items from dollar tree.

God sent me an Angel in July 1996. I met him when I was broken, lost, damaged, guards up and some. He was this nice quiet guy that I met at work. We would see each other all the time in passing and working until one day in July when I went in on a Saturday and he was there. I approached him by saying, what are you doing here on a Saturday morning. He end up saying, I'm always here the question is why are you here? I laughed, while looking all cute on purpose just in case I saw him. Knowing darn well I should have had on working clothes like I always do. I had on these cute brown jeans, with a cute top that was tucked in my pants with a belt on, this cute white sleeveless vest and hair all did up, lol. You couldn't tell me anything but I had a purpose. We end of exchanging numbers and I eventually invited him over for the first time in Oct at the time Mike Tyson was fighting. All man I feel in love with this guy after a while. I let me guards down after a while and he stole my heart. I never felt that way before. And he never talked about me or called me names just treated me like I've never been treated before. Years would go by of loving this guy until one day I found out that he was cheating then a few years later he did it again. I became very bitter and angry because I had already been there before. That stuck with me for years but for some reasons I couldn't leave him. I thought sometimes I would because we weren't married, I just couldn't. Later on in 2003 I finally said yes to marrying him because I end up asking him after I turned him down so many times. He quickly said yes and we got married in August a month later. While trying to love him, I realized I still carried that hurt and I became extremely bitter and didn't know how to let it go. So years down the road, I end up cheating in 2013 September. I was at a point where I really didn't care. It just happened, nothing I went looking for and even intended on doing. A nice conversation went wrong. I did this for 2 months until one day I said, girl you need to stop what you're doing and act like you have good sense. So one day I was on my way to DC and I detoured and said I'm going to go let this dude know I can't do this stupid thing anymore. Really did I need to go do that, absolutely not? I could have just stopped and I really didn't have to call, I owed this person nothing. Literally, the whole time there, I heard God speaking to me telling me not to go over there, go home or to DC where I should have been anyway. I get there after literally hearing and feeling that thing deep in my spirit. Talk about disobedient. Whew, was I. So I'm there and we're laughing and talking. Suddenly, I feel Quarry's presence and I get really quiet and still. Dude looks at me and say, damn you just stopped laughing, what's going on. I tell him nothing but I felt Quarry's presence and I'm thinking God tried to warn me. I end of saying, look I have to leave and I immediately left. When I got to my car there was a piece of paper on my window door. I knew it; I knew I felt Quarry's presence. I went on home and never did that again. Of course we argued for a while until one day I said to him, look you're going to either work it out or we just have to end this because I can't take this mess. I didn't leave when you did what you did and we had nothing tied together. Now you want to act like you want to keep leaving, man it was cold outside. One time I told him, you keep walking out that door and God didn't tell you to leave. In December 2013 I ask him to resign to come home and help me take care of Kelly because truthfully it was becoming very difficult when he was at work. And I had a choice, either he resign or we hire someone to come in the home. And we had already dealt with that before. In January I had a conversation with God about what am I supposed to be doing. Is it Kelly's Choice. In May I received a phone call and knew then it was Kelly's Choice because it all made good sense. I didn't realize that all along the timing was perfect, we had become so close and we loved on each other like we had just started dating. But it was so much better than before. God sealed our foundation and we became one again on a different level. A more I'm in love with each other level and supportive level. And the journey began of Edwina Wilson finding herself after all she'd been through and there was nothing but love in me and no bitterness at all. That was God working all along. See because God was really in it from the beginning when my guard was up and I soon realized that God removed them to allow Quarry to come in. He taught me how to love, and fall in love. He soon moved to Maryland with me and the kids in 1997. I couldn't believe this was really true. We had to work through a change of life there. We had some ups and downs but God had a purpose for our life and he soon healed, sealed, delivered even sealed the cracks and crevices. And today we have a solid foundation.

What made you decide to start the business that you're in?
Because of the struggles in my own journey, God gave me a dream in 2011 that instantly became a vision. I shared it with my husband after I was hysterically shaking him trying to wake him up from his sleep to ask him for a name. LOL! He woke up and I shared with him the dream because he wanted to know why I needed a name. I shared that I was in a venue that was pretty much filled to capacity. I saw wheelchairs, walkers, canes, the blind, elderly and those that cared for them. I saw myself at the podium and 3 guest speakers. We opened the podium up to those that desired to share their story, testimony or journey. I remember as I was waking up from the dream seeing the line with about 25 or more people waiting to get to the podium. I said to my husband, "what do you think about that?" He said, "Well Winnie with the people in line like that, it seems that people wanted to be heard." For me, the whole beauty of it is that he saw my vision.

I would always say that I knew God allowed me to have this dream because it was based off of raising my daughter Kelly for twenty plus years at that time, as it was the whole concept of the dream. So we talked about the name again which my husband said, "well, definitely use Kelly because of your dream." We came up with Kelly's Choice because we give her a lot of choices.

For me with Kelly's Choice I could give back and assist other care-givers of children and young adults with special needs and different abilities through some of the difficult times by sharing my own personal testimony and lessons learned. I always hope everyone will be pleased with all that Kelly's Choice has to offer and do.

With a lot of excitement I talked and shared Kelly's Choice with several people I would come in contact with out in the community. The people I would come across also fit what I would be supporting.

Though it took me three years to launch, I knew it was time because I spoke to God and I knew there were people out here that I could be a blessing to because of my journey raising my daughter. It all made sense because I love helping people. I live this life on a daily basis, I walk the life, and I wake up to it and go to sleep in this life. I feel like God knew what he was doing when I was given the dream. He knew I had a lot of experience in this business. I know what it's like to have support and not have support, and I don't take life for granted seeing my daughter every day. I have compassion and kindness and show it all the time so I feel that God has one of the most perfect people to walk in this business. And I did it!

What made you LEAP? How did you make the leap from a secure paid job to starting your own business?
What made me LEAP was my family. Knowing that people want to be heard. I experienced it first hand with my children becoming caregivers to their sister without hesitation. It allowed me to see that so many other families and people receiving care could be going through the same thing. Yet no one would ever know.

The leap from a paid job had to be done. One day I came home early from work and found my daughter home by herself because her

attendant had left her alone. I had to trust God on leaving my job because financially I knew I really couldn't afford it. At the same time I
didn't want anything to happen to my daughter as well. As a caring and
concerned mother I had to take that leap and leave. I soon realized that
it had to be done because the calling on me to be a voice to the voice-
less was too strong. So I talked to my husband and we began to get our
affairs in order to make this new venture work.

How do you balance or how did you balance your work/home life?
For me I don't think I ever found balance. Raising 4 children and one
with a disability that needed total care was all too difficult to find any
balance. Every day was different and I never knew what the next day
would bring. Sometimes I would work a full time day job, I would have
to work a night shift or an overnight shift or sometimes not have a job
at all because life and kids wouldn't allow it to happen. There were also
times I would have to take on a temp job.

However, now working from home life is a little better because I have
all young adults now and Kelly goes pretty much wherever I go. Which
is a blessing because within my business Kelly is the name behind it.
Everything we do has to do with the support of Caregivers or those that's
differently able and she fits right it. After all, it's based off her journey as
well. So it just makes since.

**What do you say to yourself when you feel like giving up? What keeps
you going?**
I honestly feel like giving up is too easy, so I would never give up. I would
press my way through and pray at the same time. I've never been one
that gives up. I have been through too much to even think about giving
up. When I think about how many times God has kept me, it's hard to
even let that thought fester in my mind.

I began to see my kids (even as young adults), my granddaughters,
and most of all Kelly in front of me and I think to myself she needs me

more than anything. If I give up who will keep her? Who will care for her like I do? Who will love her as much as I do? She is the biggest part of what keeps me going. I have always felt like I am the best fit for her, so I dedicate my time to her.

And my husband keeps me going as well, he always seems to know the right time to step in and give me those words of motivation. He keeps me lifted when he sees me feeling some kind of way. He would always tell me "I've come too far" and say, "Isn't that what you would say!"

What was the best advice you ever received? Worst advice?

My husband would always tell me that, "Everyone is not like you Winnie! So don't expect people to do what you would do or do things the way you expect them to do because that can become frustrating for you." And Ms. Jesse Mae would always tell me to be specific in what you ask for because if you don't, you're going to get what you ask for and to NEVER give up.

The worst advice ever given to me is that I have all the time in the world, so take my time. This is actually not true, time waits for no one. So if you want something you have to go forth and get it. Remember time is of the essence!

We All know the saying It takes a village to raise a child, but for a mom starting her own business, the village may be a state. So who do you turn to or go to for help? Who are your go-to people/services?

I always turn to my husband for advice, his opinion and his thoughts. I look forward to him supporting me in decisions that I come to him with. He's always my go to person. And foremost we always pray about everything.

I may go on occasions to my children and I also have a few very dependable honest people that I have grown to trust, and trust their opinions. I will call on them when the occasion calls for it.

What do you do to unwind and recharge? How important is this for a Mompreneur?

Most often my way of unwinding is with quiet times sitting in my room in a nice comfy chair at the foot of my bed with no one around. To include no TV, radio or any noise of any kind. Or I would take a ride out alone with no radio on. I've also recently added going to restaurants by myself and sit in to eat. It gives me a breath of fresh air, peace and time to re-coup, so that I can come back recharged. It also gives me time to open up and receive what God has for me.

It's very important to be able to take time for yourself because it could wear you down quickly if you don't have a break in between your everyday life, journey or duties.

What book would you recommend for a Mompreneur just starting out? Why this particular one?

I don't have any particular book that I would recommend. I would just say chose something about business that would inspire and motivate you whether it's someone's story or just going in business altogether. Something to empower you to not be afraid to leap. You would always want something that would encourage you to go after your dreams and inspirations.

What are some of the ways that you involve or have involved your family in your business?

They take part in every event we have. They are the front end in my business when we're at the venues.

They are a big part of all events that I have, like running the front desk, handling the money, answering questions, hosting, presenting, etc. They even travel with us on occasions when needed. They are well versed in all duties of the business.

What did it feel like to make your first dollar as a Mompreneur? How long did that take?

I was so proud of myself for not giving up and it felt like this is only the beginning. This is really working. I was so excited and I said, "I am going to work harder to keep it coming because the more I make the more I can help others."

Kids & Significant others, do and say the darndest things. Please share with us one of your funniest moments, embarrassing moments, saddest moments, and most rewarding moment that involving your family and your business?

Great thing to ask because with my husband we have so many great moments, a lot of laughs from things as simple as me calling him my boo thang on the radio or me patting him on the butt around a lot of people which catches him off guard.

One of my most rewarding moments with family is a moment about Kelly. After 26 years she came out of adult briefs and began wearing panties. She learned to ask to go to the bathroom, (though she still needed assistance) but she did it and is still asking. But it taught her that she can do anything she put her mind to and she was so excited just knowing that she did that. It makes life so much easier when on the road traveling for business, and at different events. Whew, to God be the Glory!

The saddest moment was when my grandmother passed at the age of 95. She was the only person that really supported me when it came to Kelly. She really loved Kelly unconditionally and didn't make a difference in her different ability. As a matter of fact when I moved from Maryland in 2006 she was so mad at me and ask me "why did I take her away from her"? Kelly and my grandmother would sit and talk for hours knowing Kelly talk a lot and repeats herself over and over my grandmother didn't allow that to stop her from caring for Kelly or keeping Kelly when I needed her to or when we would come in town to visit.

She believed in me and everything that I wanted to pursue. She would always tell me to never give up and though life may seem like its hard, it's only as hard as I make it to be. So for her not to be here, when I launched Kelly's Choice was very disappointing. I know she would have cheered me on and with that being said I know she's cheering me on anyway.

What is Your Favorite Quote?

Create the highest, grandest possible vision for your life because you become what you believe.
~ Oprah Winfrey

Leave us with ONE word to describe a Mompreneur.

Strong!

A Woman's Worth Bio

Winnie is a native of Landover, Maryland, wife of Deacon Quarry Wilson and the mother of four young adults, one in which was diagnosed with cerebral palsy, a few months after birth, her daughter, Kelly. She also has four lovely granddaughters. Winnie has managed a home, family, career, life, and the list goes on while caring for Kelly. She's also an inspiring actress that has been in several plays, commercials and films. With her strong faith in God and will power to not limit her daughter, Kelly has thrived high above the doctor's expectations. Because of the struggles within her own journey, God gave Winnie a Dream in July 2011 that became an instant Vision and Winnie founded Kelly's Choice so she could give back and assist other caregivers of children & young adults with special needs and different abilities through some of the difficult times by sharing her own personal testimony and lessons learned. She hopes that you will be pleased with all that Kelly's Choice has to offer.